ROSE GUIDE TO JOSHUA, JUDGES, AND RUTH

Rose Guide to Joshua, Judges, and Ruth

Published by Rose Publishing
An imprint of Tyndale House Ministries
Carol Stream, Illinois
rose-publishing.com

ISBN 979-8-4005-0372-6

Contributing authors: Paul H. Wright, PhD (chapter 2: *Joshua and the Conquest of Canaan;* chapter 6: *The World of Ancient Israel*); Madison C. Cannon, ThM (chapter 7: *Who's Who in Joshua, Judges, and Ruth*); chapter 3: *Judges of Israel* (Rose Publishing, 2016); chapter 4: *Life of Samson* (Rose Publishing, 2016); chapter 5: *The Story of Ruth* (Rose Publishing, 2013); chapter 8 *Twelve Tribes of Israel* (Rose Publishing, 2014)

Printed in China

31 30 29 28 27 26 25

7 6 5 4 3 2 1

CONTENTS

CHAPTER 1

Joshua, Judges, and Ruth: An Overview

"I will never leave you nor forsake you" (Josh. 1:5). This was God's promise to Joshua as he and the people of Israel waited at the edge of the promised land.

Almost forty years earlier, Joshua had been one of twelve spies whom Moses sent to scout the land of Canaan. Joshua and Caleb returned from Canaan with a favorable report for Moses, but the other ten spies persuaded the Israelites to stay out, for the people who lived in the land were big and powerful, like giants in their eyes. Joshua, however, challenged the Israelites to have courage: "The Lord is with us. Do not be afraid" (Num. 14:9). But the people listened to their fears more than God's promises. As a result, God let them wander in the wilderness for decades until that generation passed away.

The books of Joshua, Judges, and Ruth cover more than three hundred years of biblical history (c. 1406–1051), from the end of the wilderness wanderings following the exodus to just before the era of Israel's first kings.

The book of Joshua opens with a second chance for God's people. And this time, they found the courage that the earlier generation lacked; this time, they headed into Canaan to take on the giants in the land.

THE STORY OF JOSHUA, JUDGES, AND RUTH

Joshua

The entry into Canaan began with a miraculous sign of God's presence. God stopped the waters of the Jordan River so that the people could cross on dry land. This was reminiscent of the Red Sea parting when Moses and the Israelites left Egypt.

Joshua's conquest of Canaan cities also began with a miracle: God brought down the massive walls of Jericho. Rahab, a Canaanite woman in Jericho, wisely understood what was happening: "I know that the Lord has given you this land.... For the Lord your God is God in heaven above and earth below" (Josh. 2:9, 11). When Jericho fell, she and her family were spared because of her faith and assistance to Israel.

After Jericho, Joshua and his army moved through central Canaan. Near Shechem, between Mount Ebal and Mount Gerizim, Joshua and all the people assembled to worship the Lord. Shechem was the location where Abraham and his family had settled centuries earlier when God called him to migrate to Canaan (Gen. 12:6). Joshua built an altar on Mount Ebal, the priests presented offerings to the Lord, and Joshua read the law of Moses to all the people, exhorting them to obey their covenant with God.

Next, Joshua conquered cities in the southern region of Canaan, followed by victories in the north. In all these battles, God was their behind-the-scenes military commander, present and empowering (Josh. 5:13–15). Feared by the people of the land, the Israelites quickly settled throughout Canaan and Joshua allotted specific territories to the tribes of Israel. The book of Joshua closes with Joshua's farewell address in which he reminds the people to remain faithful to God as God had been faithful to them. Joshua memorably declared,

> Choose for yourselves this day whom you will serve, whether the gods your ancestors served beyond the Euphrates, or the gods of the Amorites, in whose land you are living. But as for me and my household, we will serve the LORD.
>
> JOSHUA 24:15

Joshua died at one hundred and ten years old and was buried in the promised land.

Joshua (Hippolyte Flandrin, 1856–1863)

Judges

Joshua's death left the tribes of Israel without a central leader. The Lord was supposed to be their king, but, as we read at the beginning of the book of Judges, "another generation grew up who knew neither the LORD nor what he had done for Israel" (Judg. 2:10). Moses had told the people, "Remember the LORD your God," but this new generation soon forgot (Deut. 8:18). The awesome victories of the past became distant tales.

The book of Judges portrays repeated cycles of sin and deliverance during this era.

Sin: Though Israel had conquered many key cities in Canaan, they settled alongside the remaining Canaanites in the land (Judg. 2:20–23). In ancient Near East religions, people believed that a multitude of deities ruled over all aspects of life. The Israelites often turned to these false gods instead of trusting in the one true God to provide for their needs.

Oppression: In response to Israel's sins, God allowed other nations to oppress Israel. This oppression was not a mere inconvenience; in the ancient world, it was brutal and violent. Many Israelites probably felt like the farmer Gideon when he said, "Where are all [God's] wonders that our ancestors told us about?... The LORD has abandoned us" (Judg. 6:13).

Repentance: In desperation, the Israelites eventually cried out to God: "We have sinned against you, forsaking our God and serving the Baals" (Judg. 10:10).

Deliverance: In his mercy, God would then raise up a leader (a judge) to deliver Israel from their oppressors. Notable among the twelve judges in the book of Judges are Deborah, Gideon, and Samson. Deborah was a prophet who led Israel to defeat King Jabin who "cruelly oppressed the Israelites for twenty years" (Judg. 4:3). Gideon, an ordinary farmer and "least" among his family, was called by God to lead extraordinary military victories (Judg. 6:15). Samson was a foolish and revengeful man whom God, nevertheless, empowered with amazing physical strength to accomplish God's purpose of breaking Philistine dominance over Israel.

Peace: With the success of each judge, Israel would then experience a time of peace. But eventually the Israelites would fall back into worshiping other gods, and the cycle would start again.

Interestingly, the last five chapters in the book of Judges do not include any judges. This section consists of stories about Israelite violence, idolatry, and civil war between the tribes of Israel. In addition to outside oppressors, the people of God were oppressing each other too. Why was everything so chaotic? These chapters explain, "In those days, Israel had no king and everyone did as they saw fit" (Judg. 17:6; 18:1; 21:25).

Ruth

The story of Ruth is set during a latter part of the era of the judges, a time when Israel's spiritual and social life was a mess (Ruth 1:1). Ruth's story is quite different than the stories in the book of Judges. The book of Ruth does not include amazing feats of strength like in Samson's story or shocking military victories like in Gideon's; but to the two widowed women in this story, what God did in their lives must have seemed just as miraculous.

The book begins with a famine that caused Naomi and her family to move from Bethlehem to Moab. (Moab had been an enemy of Israel; Judg. 3:12.) Naomi's husband and her two sons died in Moab, leaving her destitute. She returned to Bethlehem, but she was not alone. Naomi's daughter-in-law,

Ruth in the Fields (Hugues Merle, 1876)

Ruth, a Moabite and also a widow, chose to go with her. Ruth pledged loyalty to Naomi: "Where you go I will go, and where you stay I will stay. Your people will be my people and your God my God" (Ruth 1:16). Life in Bethlehem would not be easy for Ruth. She was a widow, childless, and a foreigner.

In Bethlehem, Ruth worked among the poor, gleaning leftovers in grain fields. But God was at work behind the scenes of her life. The field she gleaned in belonged to an Israelite named Boaz. He had heard of Ruth's unwavering dedication to Naomi, and he was moved to compassion toward Ruth. By the end of the story, Boaz, an Israelite and "a man of worth" (Ruth 2:1), is married to Ruth, a Moabite and "a woman of noble character" (Ruth 3:11). Being from the same clan as Naomi's family, Boaz acted as a "guardian-redeemer" (Ruth 2:20) and bought back Naomi's family land for her. The Lord blessed Ruth and Boaz with a son—a grandson for Naomi who renewed her life with joy. It is through this child's lineage that King David and, most importantly, Jesus the Messiah came (Matt. 1:5–6).

God's love shines through this story in the lives of ordinary people who showed extraordinary kindness and loyalty during a time when those qualities were difficult to find.

THE HISTORICAL BOOKS

Joshua, Judges, and Ruth are the first three books in a large section of the Old Testament called the Historical Books. This section comes immediately after the Pentateuch. (The Pentateuch is Genesis through Deuteronomy.)

The books in this second section of the Old Testament deal with Israel's historical experience with the land and their God. The books range from conquering, settling, and experiencing the many joys, temptations, failures, and

Historical Books

Joshua

Judges

Ruth

1 and 2 Samuel

1 and 2 Kings

1 and 2 Chronicles

Ezra

Nehemiah

Esther

challenges of dwelling in the land as the Israelites learned how to live as God's people. The books cover the history of Israel from the time of Joshua's conquest (1400s BC) to the time of Ezra and Nehemiah (400s BC). In between, we find a dramatic history of a people, their leaders, many painful disappointments, and some remarkable accomplishments. Israel changed from a loosely organized group of twelve tribes during the era of Joshua and the judges to a united kingdom under kings Saul, David, and Solomon; and then to a divided kingdom, an exiled people, and finally a returning people under leaders like Ezra and Nehemiah.

The many narratives in these books illustrate for us how God relates in history to his people and the whole world. They show how God works his will in human history.

- God works in direct ways, as in the stories of Joshua entering the promised land.
- God works in indirect ways, through Israel's judges and prophets, and also through nations like the Philistines, Assyrians, and Babylonians.
- God works behind the scenes, as in the stories of Ruth and Esther.

JOSHUA, JUDGES, AND RUTH IN BIBLICAL HISTORY

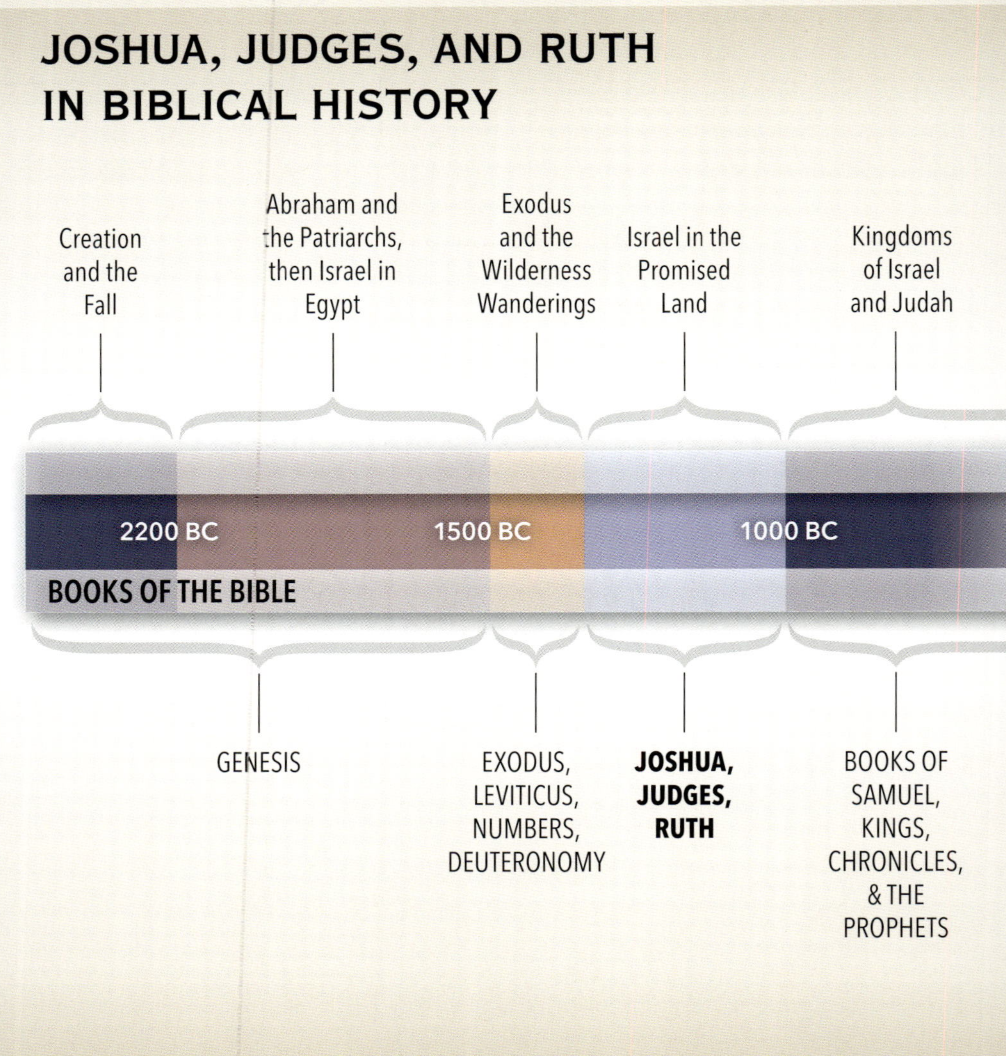

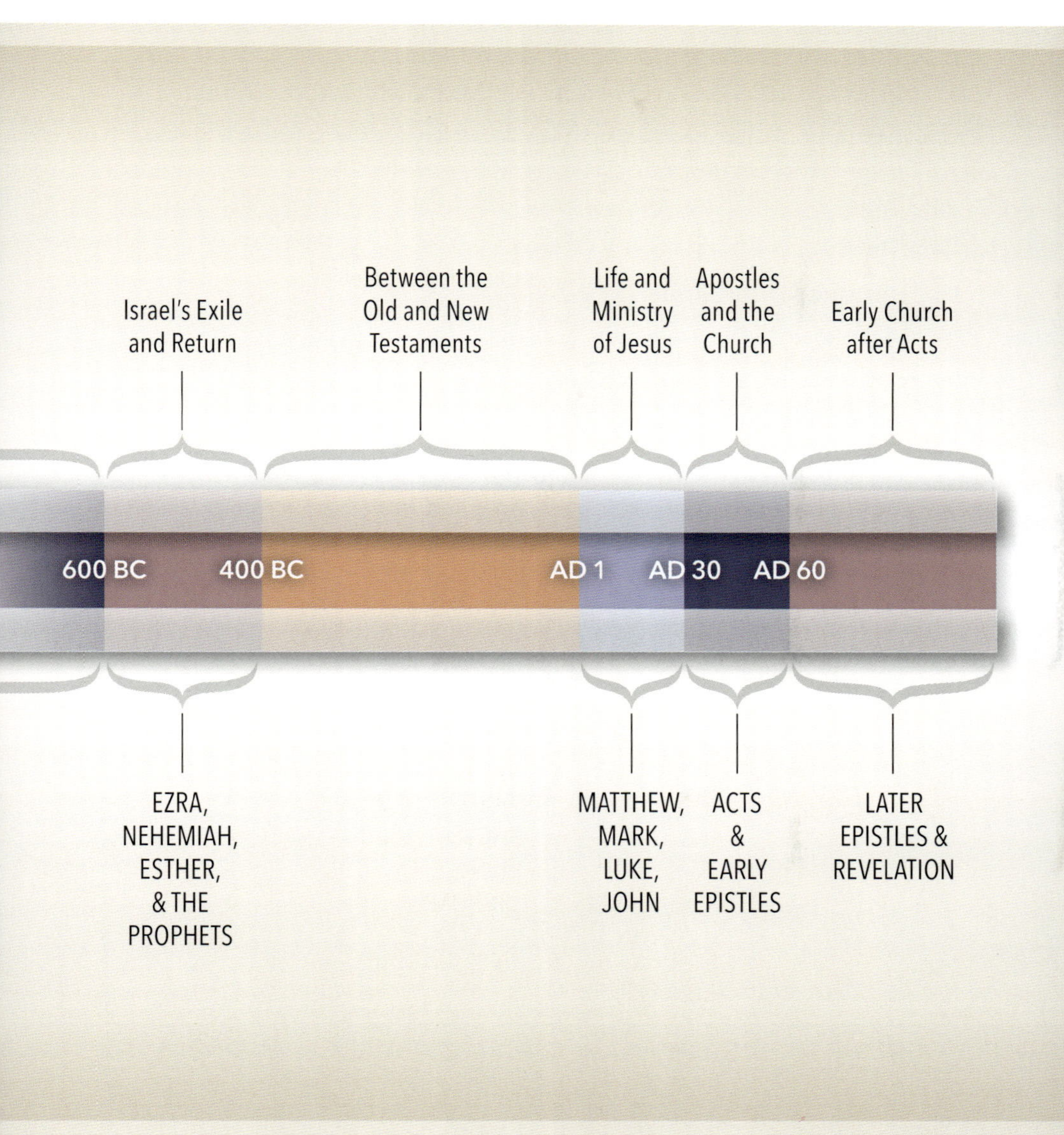
Israel's Exile and Return
Between the Old and New Testaments
Life and Ministry of Jesus
Apostles and the Church
Early Church after Acts
600 BC
400 BC
AD 1
AD 30
AD 60
EZRA, NEHEMIAH, ESTHER, & THE PROPHETS
MATTHEW, MARK, LUKE, JOHN
ACTS & EARLY EPISTLES
LATER EPISTLES & REVELATION

THE BOOK OF JOSHUA

Purpose

The book of Joshua functions as a bridge between the wilderness experience and the time in the promised land. It shows how God brought his people into the promised land and gave them rest. The book also tells the story of Joshua, whom God chose to be the leader of Israel after Moses's death.

Outline

1. Entrance into Canaan (1:1–5:12)
    a. Joshua's leadership (1)
    b. Rahab and the spies (2)
    c. Crossing the Jordan River (3:1–5:12)
2. Conquest of Canaan (5:13–12:24)
    a. Fall of Jericho (5:13–6:27)
    b. Achan's sin and the fall of Ai (7:1–8:29)
    c. Renewal of the covenant (8:30–35)
    d. Conquests in the south and north (9:1–12:24)
3. Distribution of the Land (13–21)
    a. Allotments for the tribes (13–19)
    b. Cities of refuge (20)
    c. Levite cities (21)
4. A Future for Israel (22–24)
    a. Faithfulness of the eastern tribes (22)
    b. Joshua's farewell address (23)
    c. Renewal of the covenant (24)

Author

The book does not indicate who wrote it. An ancient tradition suggests Joshua as an author and the prophet Samuel as a main author or editor, though this is highly speculative.

Date

The book was likely composed early in Israel's history (1400s–1300s BC). Some linguistic evidence indicates that it was edited later, in the era of the kings (1100s–600s BC) and perhaps even during the time of exile (500s BC).

Setting

When the Israelites came to the borders of the promised land, the political and military powerhouses of the region were Egypt and Mesopotamia, and both were in a time of transition. The Canaanite kingdoms were independent and small, without an internal organization.

Themes

- God's faithfulness to his promises
- The covenant between God and Israel
- God's holiness and judgment
- The unity of God's people
- The role of Joshua as the leader of Israel

Key Bible Verses

"Do not be afraid; do not be discouraged, for the LORD your God will be with you wherever you go" (Josh. 1:9).

"But as for me and my household, we will serve the LORD" (Josh. 24:15).

THE BOOK OF JUDGES

Purpose

The book of Judges offers a theological (or prophetic) look at the history of God's people; it contrasts God's faithfulness with humanity's unfaithfulness and fickleness. It also provides a rationale for the kings, who were supposed to care for Israel's safety, lead the people to obedience of the law, and promote the pure worship of the Lord. In the era of the judges, "Israel had no king; everyone did as they saw fit" (Judg. 21:25).

Outline

1. An Incomplete Conquest and a Failing Faith (1:1–3:6)
2. A Cycle of Sin, Punishment, and Grace (3:7–16:31)
    a. Judges Othniel, Ehud, and Shamgar (3:7–31)
    b. Judge Deborah (4–5)
    c. Judge Gideon (6–9)
    d. Judges Tola, Jair, Jephthah, Ibzan, Elon, and Abdon (10–12)
    e. Judge Samson (13–16)
3. Spiritual and Moral Decay (17–21)
    a. Micah's idols (17–18)
    b. The Levite, the concubine, and a tribal war (19–21)

Author

The book gives no indication about its author. Ancient Jewish tradition credits the prophet Samuel with having written it, though this is far from certain.

Date

Like its author, the date that the book of Judges was written also remains unknown.

Setting

The events in the book of Judges take place in various parts of Canaan where the tribes of Israel had settled, including key locations like Gaza, Bethlehem, Shechem, Gibeah, Shiloh, and Mount Tabor.

Themes

- Sin and punishment
- God's justice and mercy
- Covenant loyalty and disloyalty
- God's holiness and judgment
- The unity of God's people

Key Bible Verses

"After that whole generation had been gathered to their ancestors, another generation grew up who knew neither the LORD nor what he had done for Israel" (Judg. 2:10).

"Then the LORD raised up judges, who saved them out of the hands of these raiders" (Judg. 2:16).

Hills near Bethlehem

THE BOOK OF RUTH

Purpose

The book of Ruth presents a wonderful, concise, yet deep story of emptiness that turns into fullness; of despair into hope; of bitter sadness into joy and celebration. It shows how God turns around his people's fortunes. The book also presents the origins of King David's royal house.

Outline

1. Famine, Migration, and Death in Naomi's Family (1)
2. Boaz Meets Ruth in the Grain Fields (2)
3. Ruth Asks Boaz to be the Guardian-Redeemer (3)
4. Marriage, Birth, and Renewal in Naomi's Family (4)

Author

The author of Ruth is unknown. Jewish tradition attributes the book to the prophet Samuel, though nothing in the text indicates this.

Date

As with the author, the date of writing is also unknown.

Setting

The events took place during the era of the judges (Ruth 1:1), sometime between the death of Joshua (c. 1350 BC) and David's ascension to the throne of Israel (c. 1000 BC). Most scholars place the story in the latter part of the era of judges. The story is set during a severe famine in Israel. Naomi and her family leave Bethlehem and travel to the land of Moab to escape the famine. Moab was one of Israel's fiercest enemies.

Themes

- God's care and providence
- Loyalty, trust, and kindness
- Redemption and renewal

Key Bible Verses

"Where you go I will go, and where you stay I will stay. Your people will be my people and your God my God" (Ruth 1:16).

"May the LORD repay you for what you have done. May you be richly rewarded by the LORD, the God of Israel, under whose wings you have come to take refuge" (Ruth 2:12).

CHAPTER 2

Joshua and the Conquest of Canaan

The story of Joshua is one of personal courage, perseverance, faithfulness to God, and anticipation of a secure life at home—all in the face of immense difficulty. The first half of the book of Joshua portrays Israel's conquest of Canaan under the leadership of Joshua, while the second half focuses on Joshua's division of the land among the tribes of Israel.

WHO WAS JOSHUA?

Joshua was the son of Nun, from the tribe of Ephraim, and he became Moses's military commander after the exodus and during the forty years of wilderness wanderings. His original name was Hoshea, which means "salvation," but Moses changed his name to Joshua which means "the LORD is salvation" (Num. 13:8, 16). After Moses's death, Joshua took up the mantle and led the tribes of Israel in the conquest of Canaan. The Bible says that Joshua lived to be one hundred and ten years old and was buried in Timnath Serah, in the hill country of Ephraim (Josh. 24:29–30).

Even before the conquest of Canaan in the book of Joshua, Bible readers are introduced to Joshua as someone who is doing the kinds of things that would prepare him to bravely lead Israel into Canaan:

- As a military commander, Joshua repulsed the Amalekites in Israel's first battle after the exodus (Ex. 17:9–16).
- As a disciple, he was with Moses on Mount Sinai (Ex. 24:13; 32:15–18).
- As a spy, he was faithful and fearless, believing that Israel could take the land even though the Canaanites had strong cities (Num. 13:1–33).

Throughout the story, Joshua exhibits the same leadership qualities as Moses: He is trustworthy, competent, and devoted—and only grows in these traits after entering Canaan.

MOSES	JOSHUA
The people recognized Moses's leadership (Ex. 4:29–31).	The people acknowledged Joshua as their new leader (Josh. 1:17; 4:14).
Moses led Israel out of Egypt by the crossing of the Red Sea (Ex. 14).	Joshua led Israel into the promised land by the crossing of the Jordan River (Josh. 3–4).
Moses removed his sandals when God spoke to him through the burning bush (Ex. 3:5).	Joshua removed his sandals before God's presence (Josh. 5:13–15).
Moses was Israel's military leader during the exodus and the wilderness wanderings (Num. 21:32–35).	Joshua was Israel's military leader in the conquest of the land (Josh. 6).

WHEN DID JOSHUA LIVE?

The Bible places Joshua's conquest of Canaan 40 years after the exodus, which the book of 1 Kings says happened 480 years before the dedication of Solomon's temple (Deut. 8:2; 1 Kings 6:1). This puts the date for the conquest either around 1400 BC or 1220 BC, depending on whether the numbers 40 and 480 are best read literally or symbolically (480 may be a stylized way of saying 12 generations of 40 years each). Both ways of reading numbers were accepted methods of reckoning chronology in the ancient world.

Merneptah Stele (The Museum of Egyptian Antiquities, Cairo, Egypt)

The only firm help in dating the conquest from ancient extra-biblical texts is the Merneptah Stele. This stele is an Egyptian inscription that mentions a campaign of Pharaoh Merneptah, son of Rameses II, who subdued a people called Israel in the land of Canaan in 1207 BC. While this battle is not mentioned in the Bible, the Merneptah Stele does tell us that by the end of the thirteenth century BC,

Israel was already living in Canaan and strong enough for Egypt to recognize it as an enemy.

At Hazor, there is a massive destruction layer dating to the late thirteenth century BC, indicating the end of Canaanite presence in the city. The book of Joshua says that Joshua burned and "completely destroyed" Hazor (Josh. 11:13–14). There are also late fifteenth-century BC destruction layers at Jericho and Hazor, which may be a better fit for Joshua than the thirteenth-century destruction layer. If so, as some scholars argue, the thirteenth-century destruction at Hazor was caused by Deborah and Barak, even though the Bible does not mention that they went there (Judg. 4–5).

Perhaps the most compelling archaeological data comes from sites indicating that a non-Canaanite, rural population in the twelfth and eleventh centuries BC gradually filled the land of Canaan, moving from east to west, like the direction of Joshua's conquest.

It is important to remember, however, that most of the archaeological data for the date of Israel's entry into Canaan is ambiguous, and all of it is highly debated by scholars.

SIX THEMES IN THE BOOK OF JOSHUA

1. God desires that people live faithfully.

God formalizes what it means for Israel to live faithfully by establishing a series of covenants with them and then holding them accountable when they break these covenants. The stipulations of the covenant established at Mount Sinai during Israel's wanderings in the wilderness are expressed through instructions that God gives to Moses. These instructions (or Torah), often termed "law" in English translations, are intended to teach the people of Israel how to live and to guide them toward holiness. In receiving leadership over Israel, God tells Joshua to remember Torah: "Be strong and very courageous. Be careful to obey all the law my servant Moses gave you; do not turn from it to the right or to the left, that you may be successful wherever you go" (Josh. 1:7). As the story of Joshua unfolds, Israelites and Canaanites both have opportunities to either keep or reject covenants made with God or each other. These include covenants made by Rahab and the spies (Josh. 2), God and Israel at Mount Ebal (Josh. 8:30–35), Joshua and the Gibeonites (Josh. 9), Joshua and the tribes of Reuben, Gad, and the half-tribe of Manasseh (Josh. 22), and God and Israel at Shechem (Josh. 24).

2. The reality of judgment due to sin and wrong living.

Joshua is the agent of God's long-delayed judgment against the Canaanites, a people called Amorites in Genesis 15:16. But he is also God's agent to punish the Israelite Achan, who took plunder from Jericho against the Lord's command (Josh. 7:1–26). Joshua tells the Israelites that they, too, will be driven out of the land if they persist in living unrighteously (Josh. 23:11–16). He then follows that up by saying that indeed, "You are not able to serve the LORD" (Josh. 24:19). The rest of the Bible contains a litany of times when Joshua is proven to have been correct.

3. The need for personal choice.

God's choice of Israel does not bestow special righteousness or merit on them intrinsically. Rather it gives each person a chance to become righteous. Joshua's last words to Israel were that everyone needs to choose to serve either the Lord God or the pagan gods whom Abraham had left behind in Mesopotamia (Josh. 24:14–15; Gen 12:1–3). The generation that survives Joshua has to make the same choice that Abraham made, and every generation following must choose for themselves in the same way (Ps. 78:5–8; 2 Tim. 2:2).

4. The need to remember.

Joshua knows that each generation needs to remember the great acts of God: when he brought the Israelites out of Egypt, when he provided for them during the years of wilderness wandering, and when he brought them safely to their homeland. In order to help Israel keep these memories fresh, Joshua erects permanent stone markers at the Jordan River (Josh. 4:4–7, 20–24). The tribes of Reuben, Gad, and the half-tribe of Manasseh, who settle east of the Jordan, do the same by building an altar on their side of the river (Josh. 22:10, 24–27). At the end of his life, Joshua tells the leaders of the next generation: "You yourselves have seen …" so now "hold fast to the LORD your God, as you have until now" (Josh. 23:3–8). Then he sets up a large stone as a witness to the generations yet unborn (Josh. 24:26–28).

5. The land is God's good gift.

The land of Canaan, which becomes the land of Israel after the conquest of Joshua, is intended to be a place where the Israelites can live securely and learn how to have peace with God, each other, and the world. The book of Hebrews calls this a place of God's "rest," and notes that those who turn from God forfeit their right to that rest (Heb. 3:16–19). Hebrews goes on to speak of the land of Israel as a metaphor for a greater kind of rest—spiritual redemption and afterlife, both made possible by the work of Jesus on the cross (Heb. 4:1–11).

6. Temptations abound.

By the end of the book of Joshua, Israel has settled in the land, but many Canaanites remain, and they prove to be "snares and traps" for Israel throughout their history (Josh. 23:13). Life is never safe, even (or maybe even especially) at home. Joshua's plea that Israel "not associate with these nations that remain among you" does not mean that we should shun others but rather live in ways that are more consistent with what God wants than with what those around us are doing (Josh. 23:7). The takeaway, then, is to guard against things that pollute our hearts, our minds, and our souls.

QUESTIONS ABOUT JOSHUA'S BATTLES

Perhaps the best-known episode in the story of Joshua is the fall of Jericho—sung about in the opening stanza of a spiritual: "Joshua fit the battle of Jericho, and the walls come a-tumblin' down." This is a story of victory and freedom, one that we read and sing with relish. But as a stand-alone narrative, it also looks rather bloody. For many, the actions of Joshua, in all their violent fullness, have offered a reason not to read the Bible and even to toss out the God of the Bible in the process. And so, it is important to ask this question:

- What do the battles of Joshua say about the character of God?

Once asked, a host of related questions raise their prickly heads:

- Is God a God of vengeance, favoritism, territorial claims, and, in the words of some, ethnic cleansing?
- Do Joshua's actions give us permission to act the same way today?
- And how do we reconcile God's commands to "devote [the Canaanites] to complete destruction" (Deut. 20:17 ESV; Josh. 10:40) with the Bible's directives that Israel care for everyone who lives in their midst (Ex. 22:21; Deut. 10:19)?

Bible readers have responded to questions about the morality of Joshua's conquest in a variety of ways.

From the start, it is helpful to keep in mind that Joshua and the Israelites were not fighting for their faith or to defend it against aggressors. They were not trying to spread their faith by force of arms.

Rather, they were fighting for their existence as a people. Simply put, Israel did not fight for God; God fought for Israel.

It is also important to recognize that in the ancient world each nation claimed to have its own national deity, a warrior god who fought on behalf of (or along with) its people. The Bible describes the Lord God as a warrior, one who fights for Israel (Ex. 15:1–3; Josh. 10:14, 42; 23:3; Ps. 24:8). This suggests that God chose to reveal himself in ways that the Israelites could understand, since they lived in a world that expected everyone to have a warrior deity. Put another way, in the rough neighborhood of warrior deities, the Israelites needed language that allowed them to stand up on the block. Some scholars have used the phrase "holy war" to refer to a deity fighting on behalf of its people. Even though the Bible does not use that term, we must keep in mind that prior to the separation of religion and state in modern times, there were no *non*-holy wars. Given this, many scholars have concluded that Joshua's battles are simply a description of his life and times, with God choosing to work within fallen cultures the same way that he can choose to use individuals such as Pharaoh, Nebuchadnezzar, or Cyrus to bring about his will (Ex. 6:1; Isa. 45:1–7; Hab. 1:5–11).

It is also possible that the Bible is using hyperbole when describing the extent of Joshua's conquest. So when God commands Israel to "not leave alive anything that breathes," it means the conquest of Canaan was to be complete enough to give the Israelites a place to live, but not inclusive of every person, town, city, and village in the land (Deut. 20:16–17; Josh. 10:40–42; 11:11–15). Total victory need not

Joshua Stops the Course of the Sun (Carlo Maratta, c. 1700)

mean total annihilation, neither in Joshua's battles nor in any other war of conquest in history; rather, it speaks of breaking the will of the Canaanites to resist (Josh. 5:1; 10:1–2). Many Canaanites are killed in the story, but most capitulate, at least in enough of the land for Israel to move in and settle. In fact, at the close of Joshua much of the land is still occupied by Canaanites and other non-Israelites (Judg. 1:1–26; 14:1–4). There is no hard evidence in the story of Joshua that a mass migration of Canaanites out of the land—either forced or voluntary, as would be consistent with the term "ethnic cleansing"—actually happened.

Psalm 105:42–45 states that God gave the land of Canaan to the people of Israel so that they would have a place to keep his commandments for righteous living, and that others would come to God through Israel's example. So Joshua's conquest, however bloody, may be understood as a one-off event aimed at providing Israel with their own territory where they could attempt to form a righteous society. If so, it follows that military battles are not a necessary part of God's plan to provide security and life for his people (Ps. 147:10–11; Isa. 31:1–3; see also Josh. 11:9 where Joshua destroys the Canaanite tools of war rather than capturing and using them himself). Moreover, the Old Testament law gives specific provisions about how to fight a war, guidelines which are relatively merciful on the foe when compared to the tactics of Israel's enemies (Deut. 20:1–20). These provisions recognize that war is a part of this fallen world and God's people are expected to live in ways that are as redemptive as possible, given real-life situations (Deut. 21:10–14).

Just before the conquest of Jericho, Joshua encounters an angel of God, the commander of the Lord's army, with sword drawn for battle. Joshua asks whose side he is on. By simply replying "neither," the angel warns Joshua that he will side with whoever is holy before God (Josh. 5:14). This reveals that God is not just a national deity whose claims begin and end at territorial boundaries or with a single nation. Indeed, the creator God holds title to all lands, not just the land of Israel (Deut. 32:8). It follows that God did not reject the Canaanites because of favoritism or ethnic cleansing but because they had forfeited their rights to the land because of their sins (Gen. 15:16). Now, in Joshua, it is Israel's opportunity to show that they are worthy, but with a clear warning from God that they, too, will lose their right to live there if they disregard God's instructions—the Torah (Deut. 9:3–5; 31:9–29). This is exactly what happened with the Babylonian exile. The apostle Peter understands this when, in his conversation with Cornelius, a pagan who had come to faith in Jesus, he says "I now realize how true it is that God does not show favoritism but accepts from every nation the one who fears him and does what is right" (Acts 10:34–35).

Because God promised to give the land of Canaan to Abraham's descendants, many Bible readers view Joshua's battles in Canaan not as a war of conquest but of reconquest, not of aggression but of liberation, not of invasion but of coming home. The land, then, was fundamentally not something won by Israel but received as a gift from God. Whether Israel's gift of the land was intended to be for Bible times only or continues to have political relevance for the Middle East today is a matter of much debate.

THE STORY OF JOSHUA

The Spies (Josh. 1:1–2:24)

I know that the Lord has given you this land and that a great fear of you has fallen on us, so that all who live in this country are melting in fear because of you.

JOSHUA 2:9

The opening scene has Israel camped east of the Jordan River at a place called Shittim (Josh. 2:1). The name Shittim means "acacias," trees found throughout the desert regions of the Middle East but not the hill country of Canaan which is to become Israel's heartland home. The mention of Shittim is a subtle clue that Israel is still in the wilderness, but about to leave that stage of their journey behind as they cross the Jordan River.

The spies whom Joshua sends to survey Jericho stay in the home of Rahab, a Canaanite prostitute. Rahab appears in the genealogy of Jesus (Matt.1:5), and both Hebrews 11:31 and James 2:25 commend her for hiding the spies. Later in the Joshua story, we see that Rahab, who should have been subject to destruction along with the rest of Jericho, is instead joined to the people of Israel because of her decision to follow the God of Israel (Josh. 6:22–23). The reference that Rahab hides the spies under stalks of flax is a detail that provides historical accuracy to the story (Josh. 2:6). Flax needs a warm, wet climate to grow, and the region of Jericho, an oasis watered by a spring that flows at an average of 1,000 gallons per minute, provides exactly the right conditions for that.

When the spies return to Joshua, their report is positive, unlike the report given by the majority of spies who had scouted Canaan forty years earlier (Num. 13:25–33). The first episode of the Joshua story ends with great optimism for the tasks ahead.

The Jordan River (Josh. 3:1–5:15)

The priests who carried the ark of the covenant of the LORD stopped in the middle of the Jordan and stood on dry ground, while all Israel passed by until the whole nation had completed the crossing on dry ground.

JOSHUA 3:17

Israel's crossing of the Jordan River on dry ground echoes the crossing of the Red Sea, the receding waters of Noah's flood, and the third day of creation. In all four instances, God pushes deep water aside to prepare dry land so that his people can live. The parting of the Jordan River is also a sign that God is with Joshua as he had been with Moses (Josh. 3:7; 4:14).

Israel crosses into Canaan in the late winter and early spring, just in time to celebrate Passover (Josh. 5:10–12; see Deut. 16:1–8). This is also the time of year when the winter rains which fill the tributaries of the

Jordan make their collective way toward the Dead Sea, causing the river to flood. The banks of the river at Adam, twenty miles (thirty-two km) north of Jericho, are crumbly, and the erosive power of the Jordan's floodwaters has been known in historic times to collapse them and temporarily block the water's flow. As when God used a strong wind to blow back the waters of the Red Sea, so he seems to use natural means to halt the waters of the Jordan.

After crossing the Jordan River, Joshua sets up twelve stones at Gilgal as a memorial marking Israel's miraculous crossing. Each stone was taken from the river and represents one of the twelve tribes of Israel (Josh. 4:4–9, 20). It was a common practice in the ancient Near East to erect standing stones to mark notable events, signify treaties between nations or people, or honor a deity (Gen. 28:18; 31:45–50; Deut. 27:2–4). These standing stones were intended to remain as witnesses for future generations.

The Israelites complete their journey across the Jordan River on the tenth day of the first month, the same day that God commanded them to choose their sacrificial lamb for Passover back in Egypt (Josh. 4:19; Ex. 12:1–3). Joshua's first act in Israel's new land is to circumcise all the males who had been born during their forty-year journey, formally bringing everyone into God's covenant and indicating that their long life in pagan Egypt is a thing of the past. They celebrate the Passover meal four days later. The daily supply of manna, which had sustained Israel throughout their forty years in the wilderness, stops the very next day. Everyone is now safely home.

At a critical juncture in the story, Joshua meets the "commander of the army of the LORD" outside Jericho. When asked what message the commander brings, he replies with a directive: "Take off your sandals, for the place where you are standing is holy" (Josh. 4:14). Israel will come to understand that their entire land, not just this Jericho gateway, belongs to God and is therefore holy (Ps. 78:54). Israel's upcoming settlement in the land is akin to living in God's sanctuary, or temple (Ex. 15:17). Like Moses's encounter at the burning bush, this episode in Joshua tells the reader that God is the one in charge: He can neither be controlled nor compelled to do anyone's will other than his own.

The Fall of Jericho (Josh. 6:1–27)

When the trumpets sounded, the army shouted, and at the sound of the trumpet, when the men gave a loud shout, the wall collapsed; so everyone charged straight in, and they took the city.

JOSHUA 6:20

The account of the conquest of Jericho is not so much a military victory as it is a sacred endeavor. For six days the Israelite army marches once around the city, their procession led by priests carrying the ark of the covenant, an elaborately decorated, gold-plated box representing the presence of God. On the seventh day, they circle Jericho seven times, with the city's walls falling at the sound of their shouts and trumpet blasts. Clearly the author intends for us to understand this as a miracle of God, timed to echo the six days of creation culminating in the fullness of the seventh day.

Like a burnt offering, the city is devoted, or given, to God, then consumed by fire. The Hebrew word translated "devoted" is *herem* (Josh. 6:17). This word usually refers to something devoted for God's use only (Josh. 6:17–18; 10:28, 35, 37, 39–40; 11:11–12, 20–21). By implication, something devoted is banned for use by people. In the account of Jericho's destruction, the city is given to God as the firstfruit of victory, and the Israelites are banned from rebuilding it and living there (Josh. 6:26–27).

The Defeat of Ai (Josh. 7:1–8:35)

Do not be afraid; do not be discouraged. Take the whole army with you, and go up and attack Ai. For I have delivered into your hands the king of Ai, his people, his city and his land.

JOSHUA 8:1

Jericho is the eastern gateway to several routes climbing into the hill country, each of which leads to a strong Canaanite city: from north to south Bethel, Gibeon, and Jerusalem. Joshua chooses the route through Bethel, with the goal of reaching mounts Gerizim and Ebal, where Moses had instructed Israel to renew the covenant (Deut. 11:26–32). These mountains flank the great tree of Moreh near Shechem, where Abraham had built his first altar, giving Israel ancestral rights to the region of Canaan (Gen. 12:6–7; Gen. 33:18–20). Joshua's chosen route leads through Bethel and Ai. It is likely that Ai was not a proper city at the time but an eastern outpost guarding Bethel, the main Canaanite city of the region. The Hebrew word for city can be used for any fortified location no matter how large or how small. Scholars debate the exact location of Ai, with the majority favoring the ruins at et-Tell and others preferring nearby Khirbet el-Maqatir. While Khirbet el-Maqatir has archaeological remains more consistent with Joshua's story, et-Tell sits on a better natural route to guard Joshua's advance.

The remains shown here at et-Tell are either a temple (more likely) or a palace (less likely). They date to the third millennium BC, a millennium prior to Joshua. The ruins would have been visible in Joshua's day. Ai and et-Tell both mean "ruin." (Photo by Alex Ostrovski/Wikimedia)

Due to the overconfidence of the spies Joshua had sent to Ai, the Israelites are driven back from their first attempt to overrun its garrison. Thirty-six Israelites fall in battle out of a force of "about three thousand" who went to fight (Josh. 7:3–4). While tragic, a loss of just over one percent of the fighting force should not have been enough so that "the hearts of the people melted in fear and became like water" (Josh. 7:5). It is more likely that the Hebrew term *eleph*, often translated as *thousand*, here means *units of fighting men*; the word can be translated either way, depending on the context. If so, then Joshua's initial force numbered not three thousand but perhaps only sixty to seventy-five, of which thirty-six killed in battle may be more than half.

After the battle, the reason for Israel's defeat is discovered: Achan, of the tribe of Judah, had violated the ban on profiting from the conquest of Jericho by plundering valuable goods from the city. Even though the actual theft is committed by an individual, God holds all Israel guilty. To purge the sin from everyone else, Achan's entire family is executed and his belongings destroyed. While it seems that Achan's family must have been complicit in the theft (nothing is secret in the confines of a tent), a larger factor was probably at play—that of tribal society. The smallest functional unit in tribal society is not the individual but the family, with questions of innocence, guilt, honor, and shame residing—and being dealt with—at the family level.

For the second attack, Joshua positions his main army behind the outpost of Ai. He ambushes the place from behind while the garrison of Ai chases after a decoy, a much smaller frontal assault. This time the Israelites are successful.

After defeating Ai and Bethel, Joshua fulfills Moses's command by taking all Israel to mounts Gerizim and Ebal. There he builds an altar and renews the covenant. The blessings and curses that the tribes recite to each other from the slopes of Gerizim and Ebal are probably those recorded in Deuteronomy 27–28.

Joshua's Conquest of Canaan

The South (Josh. 9:1–10:43)

All these kings and their lands Joshua conquered in one campaign, because the LORD, the God of Israel, fought for Israel.

JOSHUA 10:42

The next place to fall is Gibeon, a powerful Canaanite city that controls a strategic crossroads in the central hill country. Because the Gibeonites know they are up next, they decide that their best tactic for survival is to switch allegiance rather than fight. Their ploy—seductive and effective—is to pretend to be needy travelers from a faraway land, appealing to Israel's religious obligation to care for strangers in their midst. Joshua makes a covenant with the Gibeonites and comes under intense opposition from his own people for it. But having just ratified Israel's own covenant at mounts Gerizim and Ebal, Joshua knows the importance of the greater party keeping its promises, even if the lesser party (be it Gibeon to Israel or Israel to God) violates the terms.

Now subject to a covenant with Israel and, by implication, Israel's covenant with God, the Gibeonites became woodcutters and water carriers for the altar. While most scholars understand this to be a servile role within Israelite society, it was also a way of instilling Torah-values in the Gibeonites through loyalty to the tabernacle, the center of worship.

The neighboring Canaanite cities regard the Gibeonites as collaborators with the enemy and so try to pressure them into breaking their alliance with Israel. Jerusalem is most at risk since it lies closest to Gibeon and because Joshua now controls its best access points for expansion and economic vitality. Joshua defeats the five-city coalition led by Jerusalem directed at forcing Gibeon to come return to the Canaanite side. In doing so, he controls the perimeters of what will become the land of the tribe of Judah and, eventually, the Southern Kingdom of Judah.

As the Israelites chase the Canaanites back to their own cities, "the sun stood still [literally 'ceased'], and the moon stopped" so that the rout could be completed that same day (Josh. 10:13 ESV). Some scholars understand this as a supernatural slowing of the earth's rotation. Most suggest more natural explanations: the day seemed long because the sky was darkened by hail or an eclipse, or the darkened sky allowed Israel to beat the heat and fight more efficiently, accomplishing in one day what normally would take longer.

The North (Josh. 11:1–12:24)

They came out with all their troops and a large number of horses and chariots—a huge army, as numerous as the sand on the seashore. All these kings joined forces … to fight against Israel.

JOSHUA 11:4–5

Archaeological excavations show that Hazor, a northern city, was by far the largest in Canaan, rivaling the cities of Mesopotamia in size, strength, importance, and wealth. The name of its king, Jabin, was a common name known from ancient cuneiform texts found at Hazor. The Canaanite cities that join King Jabin to make a stand against Joshua each represent a strategic region and route leading into Galilee. Their immediate response to Jabin's beck and call confirms the Bible's description of Hazor as "the head of all these kingdoms" (Josh. 11:10).

Apparently knowing Joshua's success in unconventional warfare, Jabin's army and chariot corps gather at the Waters of Merom. Scholars identify this as either the then-swampy Huleh Valley northeast of Hazor or an area of springs in the high hills of upper Galilee to the northwest. Because chariots cannot operate in either place, it seems that Jabin wants to hide his forces behind Hazor in order to lure Joshua into the city from the south and then attack after he lowers his guard. Instead, Joshua attacks Jabin "suddenly" (Josh. 11:7), in surprise, at the Waters of Merom where his ground forces have the advantage over

Jabin's chariots. Joshua then routes Jabin's forces farther north before turning back to burn Hazor. The details of the story fit the geography of the region perfectly.

Joshua 11:13 notes that of all the places that Joshua conquered which are "cities built on their mounds," only Hazor is burned. The Hebrew word for mound is *tel*, a landscape feature formed from the ruins of cities built on top of each other over the course of many centuries. Archaeologists have found that an extensive fire destroyed Hazor in the late thirteenth century BC. Over a small part of its remains, rudimentary structures were constructed that are consistent with those of Israel settling down. Eighty percent of the surface area of Canaanite Hazor was never built on again.

Joshua 12 lists the thirty-one defeated kings and the cities where they ruled. This list serves as a map of territory that will later come under the control of Israel during the days of kings David and Solomon. While Joshua's military campaigns serve to lay claim to this territory, much of the land will remain outside of Israel's control for many generations.

The Land (Josh. 13:1–22:34)

So the LORD gave Israel all the land he had sworn to give their ancestors, and they took possession of it and settled there. ... Not one of all the LORD's good promises to Israel failed; every one was fulfilled.

JOSHUA 21:43, 45

This section of the book of Joshua contains descriptions of the territories where each tribe will settle. Sometimes these descriptions are lists of cities, sometimes they designate tribal boundaries, and sometimes they are both. The information is detailed, technical, and a tough go for most Bible readers, but it is critical to the story of Joshua for several reasons:

- These chapters show that God's promise that the descendants of Abraham, Isaac, and Jacob will inherit the land of Canaan is being fulfilled (Ps. 105:5–11).
- They also demonstrate that a specific place to call home is an important marker of Israelite identity. Land and people belong together.

Joshua and the priest Eleazar (son of Aaron) apportion land to the tribes from the Israelite religious and political center of Shiloh, where the tabernacle (the tent of meeting) is set up (Josh.18:1; 19:51). This joint effort by the political head (Joshua) and the religious head (Eleazar) shows that in the early days of settlement national leadership was unified. The two strongest institutions in every nation in the ancient world were the palace and the temple, with kings and priests usually jostling for dominance over each other.

Joshua's friend Caleb receives a special inheritance within the borders assigned to the tribe of Judah. Caleb is a Kenizzite, a tribal group already living in Canaan (Josh. 14:6, 14; see Gen. 15:18–21). We do not know how, but Caleb was so closely associated with the Israelites in Egypt that Moses chose him to represent Judah's tribe among the spies sent into Canaan, even though he was not related by blood (Num. 13:1–16). Caleb asks Joshua for an inheritance specific to him and Joshua gives him Hebron, a city in the center of Judah's territory, near the plot of ground Abraham had purchased as the family burial place (Gen. 49:28–33; Josh. 14:6–15). Caleb's inclusion in the people of Israel is a testimony that all nations will be blessed through Abraham (Gen. 12:3).

Joshua appoints six cities of refuge at strategic places throughout the land where Israelites who accidentally kill someone can flee for safety from the victim's avengers (Josh. 20:1–9; Num. 35:9–28). Three are in Canaan and three are in lands given to the tribes east of the Jordan River. Their distribution at easily accessible, central locations gives equal opportunity to everyone in need of refuge. Together, they offer a practical outworking of Torah principles that place a high value on preserving life.

To the tribe of Levi, Joshua appoints forty-eight cities that are scattered among the tribes, though most are on frontiers or in areas in close contact with Canaanite centers (Josh. 21:1–42; Num. 35:1–8). These cities, rather than a single bounded territory, are the inheritance of the Levites, who serve as priests for all Israel. In this way, priestly influence and Torah-teaching are distributed throughout the land, though focused in areas where Israel will most easily come into contact with foreigners.

Interestingly, the tribes of Reuben, Gad, and the half-tribe of Manasseh receive their inheritance east of the Jordan River, outside the borders of Canaan. This land is especially suitable for their lifestyle as livestock herders (Josh. 13:8–32; Num 32:1–42). Joshua is worried that this geographical separation will make these tribes less Israelite in their values and actions, threatening tribal unity. For this reason, when they build an altar by the Jordan River, Joshua interprets it as a rival to the tabernacle in Shiloh. The three tribes reassure Joshua that their altar is intended only to be a witness to the mighty acts of God for the next generation (Josh. 22).

Jordan River Valley in northern Israel

The Tribes of Israel

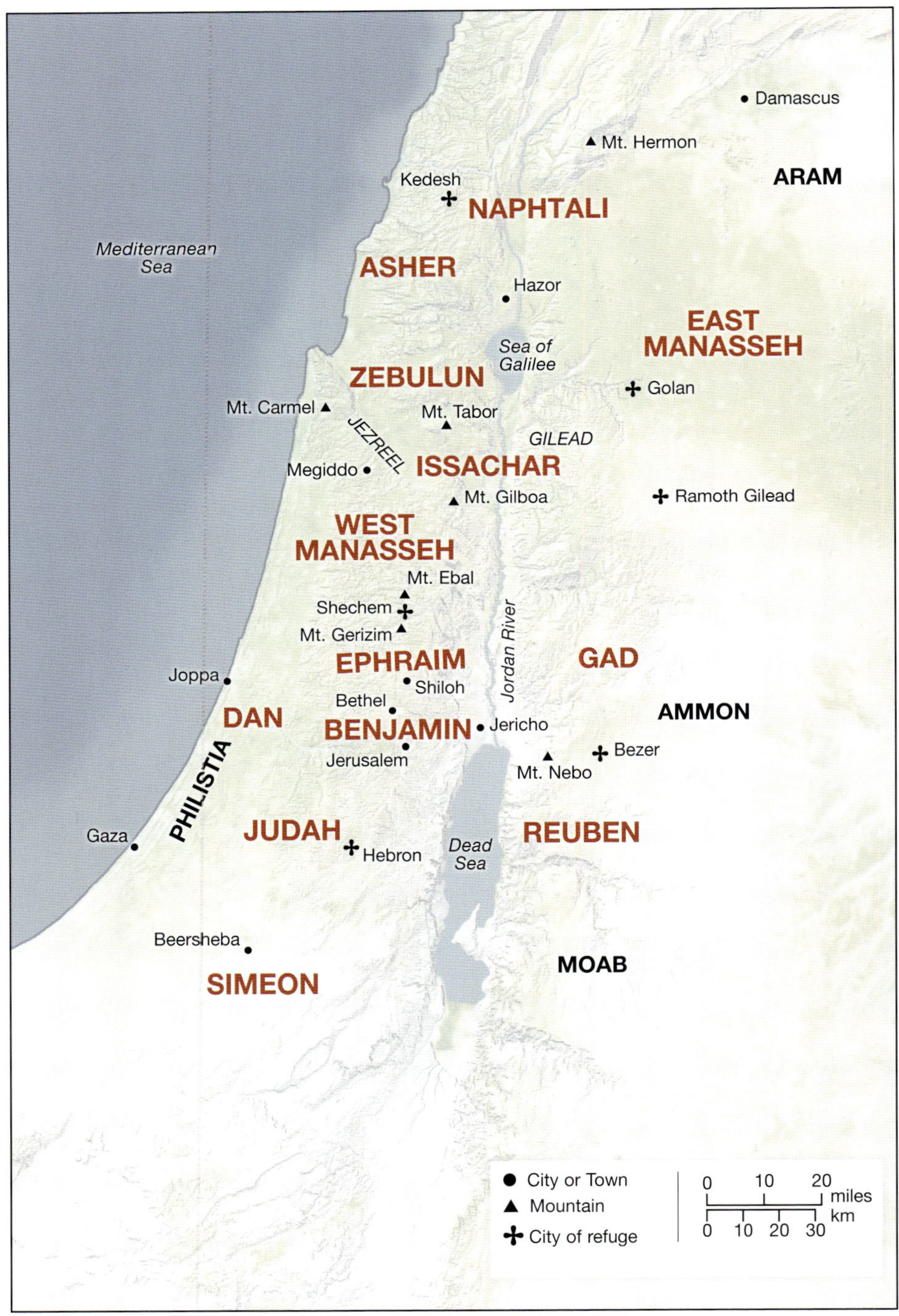

Joshua's Farewell (Josh. 23:1–24:33)

Now fear the LORD and serve him with all faithfulness. Throw away the gods your ancestors worshiped beyond the Euphrates River and in Egypt, and serve the LORD.

JOSHUA 24:14

At the opening of the story of Joshua, God tells Joshua that he must be strong and courageous for the challenging work ahead (Josh. 1:6). Now in his last days, Joshua passes this same command to all Israel: "Be very strong; be careful to obey all that is written in the Book of the Law of Moses, without turning aside to the right or to the left" (Josh. 23:6). Joshua's words of encouragement, even though he knows that Israel will fail, are his last will and testament.

Joshua puts the most essential choice before Israel: "Choose for yourselves this day whom you will serve." Will it be the gods of Abraham's ancestors beyond the Euphrates River? Will it be the gods of the Canaanites? Or will it be the Lord God of Israel? Joshua makes his choice: "As for me and my household, we will serve the LORD" (Josh. 24:15). Knowing the indecisive hearts of his people, Joshua sets up a large stone as "a witness against you if you are untrue to your God" (Josh. 24:27), and then he sends them back to their respective homes.

Joshua's story concludes with the death and burial notices of Joshua the general and Eleazar the priest. They, and Joseph's bones that the Israelites had brought with them from Egypt, are buried within the tribal inheritance of Ephraim and Manasseh, the sons of Joseph, Jacob's favorite son.

CHAPTER 3

Judges of Israel

They were not what anyone would call conventional leaders. One had a violent temper. One was the son of a prostitute. One was a woman in a male-dominated society. Another was a neglectful father. But they were also courageous, shrewd, relentless, and passionate seekers of the Lord. The Bible calls them *judges*. They were God's deliverers, chosen to liberate his people from oppression and bring his people back into a right relationship with him.

There are many lessons that can be gleaned from the judges, but perhaps the most important for us today is that no matter how often or how far we stray, God always provides a way for us to be reconciled with him. God does not give up on those who belong to him.

AN ERA OF TURMOIL

After Moses's death, Joshua completed the journey of leading God's people into the promised land. Over time, Joshua and the generation of people who had seen God's great works in securing the land passed away. This left God's people without a single, central leader.

The Israelites repeatedly fell into idolatry, worshiping the false gods of neighboring nations. In response, God allowed various enemies to oppress them. It was a brutal time of war with outside enemies and internal strife among the tribes. The Bible describes this period as being void of spiritual leadership: "In those days Israel had no king; everyone did as they saw fit" (Judg. 17:6). Indeed, the book of Judges showcases the corruption of humankind through some of the most violent stories in the Bible.

After a period of oppression, the Israelites would reach a breaking point where they would cry out for God to save them. In his time and from his mercy, God would raise up deliverers to rescue his people. This era of the judges—and the cycle of turning from God, being defeated, crying out to God, and being delivered—lasted more than three hundred years until the first king of Israel was put in place.

Cycle Pattern in the Book of Judges

JUDGES Q&A

What was the role of a judge?

The main verbs associated with the judges are "to judge" and "to deliver." The judges in the Bible had to acknowledge (judge) that the people had wandered away from God, and then rescue (deliver) the people from the consequences of their sins.

How many judges were there?

Though no one knows for certain how many judges God raised up during this period of biblical history, there are twelve judges identified in the book of Judges, plus two in the book of 1 Samuel. Some judges, like Samson and Gideon, have lengthy stories in the Bible, giving us insight into their lives and motivations. But others, like Shamgar and Elon, have only a handful of Bible verses dedicated to them, giving us just the bare facts.

In what ways did God's people disobey?

The Bible does not always state exactly how the people strayed in each instance. However, before the first judge, Othniel, we are told that the Israelites married into the families of neighboring nations and served their gods (Judg. 3:1–6). This practice of intermarrying and worshiping idols was repeated by God's people. The book of Judges notes how they served the Baals, Ashtoreths, Asherahs, and the gods of Aram, Sidon, Moab, the Amorites, and the Philistines (Judg. 3:7; 10:6).

How were the people oppressed?

Other nations in the land—such as the Philistines, Moabites, and Canaanites—dominated the Israelites. They suffered physical, economic, social, and religious oppression. These periods of oppression (one as long as forty years) had lasting effects on the people.

What does it mean when "the Spirit of the Lord came upon" someone in the Old Testament?

Many of the judges are described as having "the Spirit of the LORD come upon" them (Judg. 3:10; 6:34; 11:29; 15:14). In the Old Testament, people were not permanently filled with the Holy Spirit as believers in Jesus are today. Instead, God would allow the Spirit to temporarily enable people to accomplish extraordinary tasks to fulfill God's purposes.

Locations of the Judges

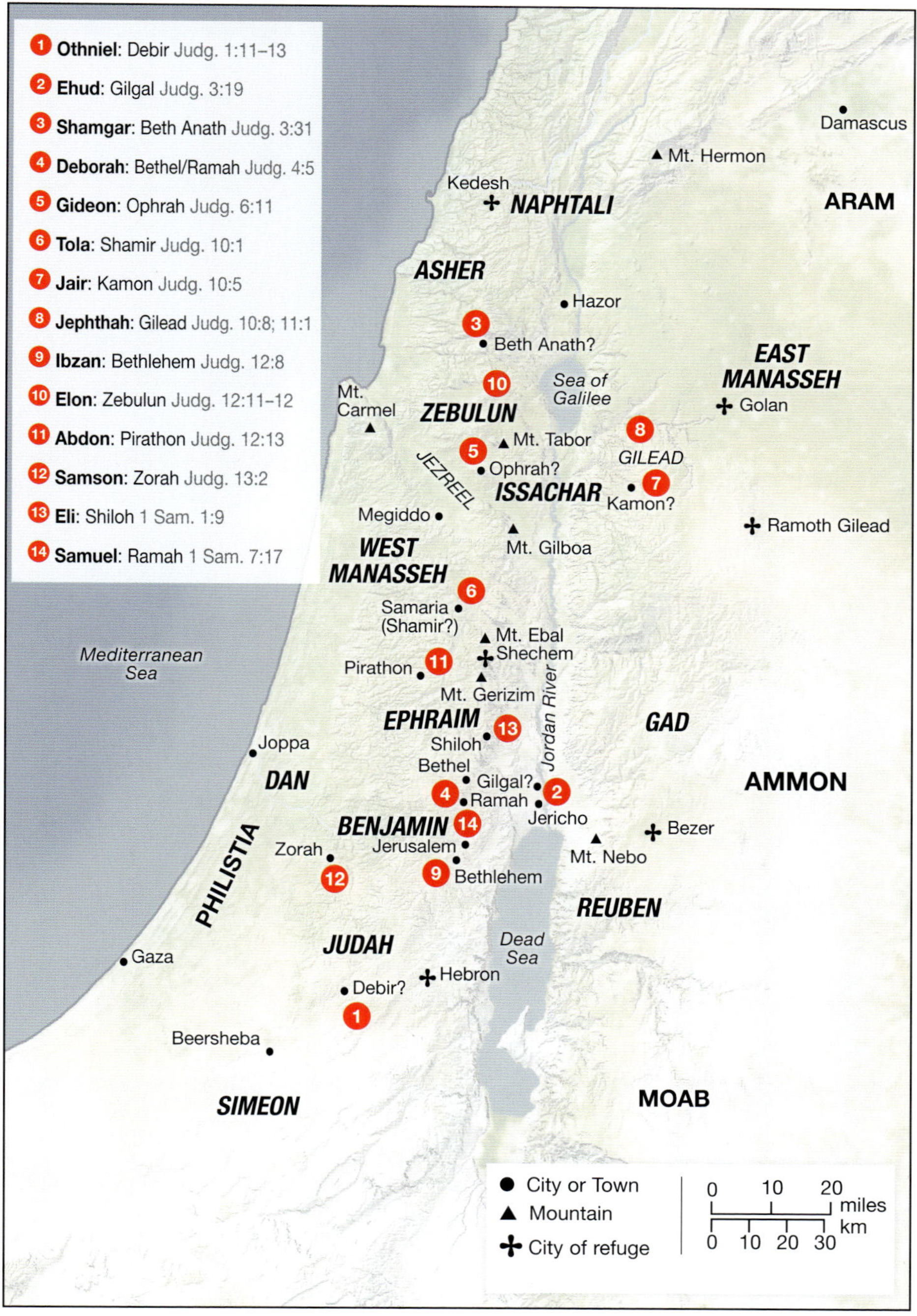

	JUDGE	MEANING OF NAME	SCRIPTURE
1	**Othniel** | *The First Judge*	Lion of God	Judges 3:7–11 (1:12–14)
2	**Ehud** | *The Left-Handed Judge*	Strong	Judges 3:12–30
3	**Shamgar** | *The One-Verse Judge*	Cupbearer	Judges 3:31
4	**Deborah** | *The Female Judge*	Bee	Judges 4:1–5:31
5	**Gideon** | *The Valiant Judge*	A cutting down	Judges 6:1–8:32
6	**Tola** | *The Hill Country Judge*	Scarlet	Judges 10:1–2
7	**Jair** | *The "30" Judge*	The Lord enlightens	Judges 10:3–5
8	**Jephthah** | *The Vowing Judge*	He opens	Judges 10:6–12:7
9	**Ibzan** | *The Marrying Judge*	Splendid	Judges 12:8–10
10	**Elon** | *The Decade-long Judge*	Oak	Judges 12:11–12
11	**Abdon** | *The Grandfather Judge*	Service	Judges 12:13–15
12	**Samson** | *The Foolish Judge*	Distinguished / Sun	Judges 13:1–16:31
13	**Eli** | *The Neglectful Judge*	Exalted is the Lord	1 Samuel 1:1–4:18
14	**Samuel** | *The Transitional Judge*	Heard of God	1 Samuel 1; 3; 7–13; 15–16; 25:1; 28

TRIBE	ENEMY	YEARS OF OPPRESSION	YEARS OF SERVICE/PEACE
Judah	Mesopotamians	8	40
Benjamin	Moabites	18	80
Unknown	Philistines	Unknown	Unknown
Ephraim	Canaanites	20	40
Manasseh	Midianites	7	40
Issachar	Unknown	Unknown	23
Manasseh	Unknown	Unknown	22
Manasseh	Philistines and Ammonites	18	6
Judah	Unknown	Unknown	7
Zebulun	Unknown	Unknown	10
Ephraim	Unknown	Unknown	8
Dan	Philistines	40	20
Levi	Family strife	Unknown	40
Levi	National strife	Unknown	Possibly 40

Years of Oppression is the time period when God allowed the Israelites to be to overpowered by their enemies. Years of Service/Peace is the time period when God raised up a judge to lead the Israelites to defeat their oppressors and bring peace to the land.

1. Othniel – The first judge

Judges 1:12–14; 3:7–11

The problem: The people of Israel did evil in the sight of the Lord.

The penalty: God allowed them to be oppressed by Cushan-Rishathaim, king of Aram (Mesopotamia), for eight years.

The petition: When the Israelites cried out to God, he raised up Othniel, the nephew of Caleb, to deliver them. (Caleb and Joshua were the only two men who had given encouraging reports when twelve men were sent by Moses to spy out the land of Canaan which they were to inherit; Num. 13.)

The provision: Othniel was victorious, and Israel had forty years of peace.

2. Ehud – The left-handed judge

Judges 3:12–30

The problem: The people of Israel did evil in the sight of the Lord.

The penalty: God allowed them to be oppressed by Eglon, king of Moab, for eighteen years.

The petition: When the Israelites cried out to God, he raised up Ehud, a left-handed Benjamite, to deliver them.

The provision: Ehud delivered a present and a secret message to Eglon. The secret message was a dagger to the belly that killed Eglon. Ehud and the people of Israel were victorious over the men of Moab, and Israel had peace for eighty years.

Ehud Kills Eglon (Teofilo Torri, c. 1608)

3. Shamgar – The one-verse judge

Judges 3:31

Shamgar killed six hundred Philistines with an oxgoad (a pointed stick used to manage cattle). In the one Bible verse that tells Shamgar's story, there is no mention of how long Israel was oppressed or how long he led Israel.

4. Deborah – The female judge

Judges 4:1–5:31

The problem: The people of Israel did evil in the sight of the Lord.

The penalty: God allowed them to be oppressed by Jabin, king of Canaan, for twenty years.

The petition: They came to Deborah, a prophet and judge.

The provision: Deborah called upon Barak and told him to assemble an army because God would deliver to him Sisera, the captain of Jabin's army. Barak refused to go unless Deborah went also. She agreed but told him that the Lord would "deliver Sisera into the hands of a woman" (Judg. 4:9). When Barak's army was victorious over Sisera's army, Sisera fled, but he encountered a woman named Jael who killed him by driving a tent peg into his head. Deborah and Barak sang a song of praise to the Lord, and Israel had rest for forty years.

Was Barak a Judge?

Although often thought to be a judge because of his association with the judge Deborah, Barak is never cited as a judge in the Bible. He is a military leader whom God teamed with Deborah for a specific battle.

5. Gideon – The valiant judge

Judges 6:1–8:32

The problem: The people of Israel did evil in the sight of the Lord.

The penalty: God allowed them to be oppressed by the Midianites for seven years.

The petition: When the Israelites cried out to God, he sent a prophet who urged them to remember God's past deliverances and rebuked them for not obeying God's voice.

The provision:

- *Gideon's first sign:* An angel appeared to a man named Gideon to tell him that he was to deliver Israel from the Midianites. Unsure of all this, Gideon requested a sign, which the angel gave him by causing fire to appear.
- *Gideon's task:* Gideon obeyed the Lord and destroyed an altar of Baal, then built a new altar to God. The people of Israel, the Midianites, and Amalekites all wanted to kill Gideon.
- *Gideon's next signs:* Gideon assembled an army and asked the Lord for a second sign. God provided the sign, but Gideon asked for yet another sign. God provided the sign again.
- *Gideon's army:* God reduced Gideon's army from 32,000 fighters to only 300, so that the people would not think they won the battle by their own power. Astonishingly, Gideon's small army was victorious!

Who Was Abimelek?

Abimelek was one of Gideon's sons who usurped power by murdering seventy of his brothers (Judg. 8:33–9:57). He convinced the people of Shechem to declare him king but later slaughtered its inhabitants and destroyed the city to quell a rebellion. Abimelek received a fatal injury when a woman in a city that he was attacking dropped a millstone on his head from a tower. The Bible explains, "Thus God repaid the wickedness that Abimelek had done to his father by murdering his seventy brothers" (Judg. 9:56).

- *Gideon's snare:* The people wanted to make Gideon their king, but he refused. However, he made a gold ephod (a religious object), and the people of Israel foolishly worshiped it instead of God, so it became "a snare to Gideon and his family" (Judg. 8:27). Yet Israel had peace for forty years.

6. Tola – The hill country judge

Judges 10:1–2

All we know of Tola is that he was the son of Puah and the grandson of Dodo of the house of Issachar, and he lived in Shamir in the hill country of Ephraim. Tola led Israel for twenty-three years.

7. Jair – The "30" judge

Judges 10:3–5

All we know about Jair is that he was from Gilead, and he had thirty sons who rode thirty donkeys and his sons ruled over thirty cities. Jair led Israel for twenty-two years.

8. Jephthah – The vowing judge

Judges 10:6–12:7

The problem: The people of Israel did evil in the sight of the Lord.

The penalty: God allowed them to be oppressed by the Philistines and Ammonites for eighteen years.

The petition: When they cried out to God, he reminded them of his past deliverances and rebuked them for not obeying his voice. At first, the Lord refused to deliver them again, but the people turned back to him, and he became sympathetic to their suffering.

The provision:

- *Jephthah's return:* Jephthah—whose father was Gilead and his mother a prostitute—was expelled from his home by his brothers. When Ammon began to attack the people of Gilead, the elders persuaded Jephthah to return and lead their army.

- *Jephthah's foolish vow:* Jephthah vowed to God that if God would give him victory, whatever first came out of his door upon his return from battle would be presented as a burnt offering. Jephthah was victorious, and when he returned home he was met by his only child, a daughter. He was distraught, but at his daughter's insistence he allowed her two months to mourn and then carried out his vow. Jephthah led Israel for six years.

The Daughter of Jephthah
(Alexandre Cabanel, 1879)

9. Ibzan – The marrying judge

Judges 12:8–10

All we know about Ibzan is that he was from Bethlehem and married his sixty sons and daughters to individuals outside his clan. Ibzan led Israel for seven years.

10. Elon – The decade-long judge

Judges 12:11–12

All we know about Elon is that he was from Zebulun, and he led Israel for ten years.

11. Abdon – The grandfather judge

Judges 12:13–15

All we know about Abdon is that he was from Pirathon in Ephraim and had forty sons and thirty grandsons, and together they rode seventy donkeys. Abdon led Israel for eight years.

12. Samson – The foolish judge

Judges 13:1–16:31

The problem: The people of Israel did evil in the sight of the Lord.

The penalty: God allowed them to be oppressed by the Philistines for forty years.

The petition: Unlike other times, the book of Judges does not say that the people cried out to God for deliverance in this instance.

The provision:

- *Samson's birth:* An angel announced to Manoah's wife that she would conceive a son who would be a Nazirite and deliver the people from the Philistines. She named her son Samson.
- *Samson's violent feud:* As Samson traveled to a neighboring city to marry a Philistine woman, he broke his Nazirite vow by eating honey from a beehive in the carcass of a lion he had killed earlier with his bare hands. Later, Samson lost a foolish bet, so he killed thirty Philistines to take their goods to pay off his debt. When Samson's wife was given to another man in marriage, Samson burned the Philistines' grain fields as revenge. The Philistines in turn burned to death Samson's wife and her father. Samson then killed one thousand Philistines with the jawbone of a donkey.
- *Samson and Delilah:* Samson fell in love with a woman named Delilah, whom the Philistines paid to discover the source of his super strength. Samson eventually revealed to her that cutting his hair (forbidden by his Nazirite vow) would make him weak. Delilah had his hair cut while he slept. When the Philistines attacked, Samson did not realize that he had lost his strength, and he was easily captured.
- *Samson's death:* The Philistines blinded and imprisoned Samson—but all the while his hair began to grow back. When thousands of Philistines were assembled together in the temple of their god, the rulers brought in Samson for the people to mock. Samson

made his way to two pillars that held up the entire structure. He prayed to God to restore his strength one last time. God granted his prayer, and Samson pushed the pillars, bringing down the temple, killing himself and thousands of Philistines.

13. Eli – The neglectful judge

1 Samuel 1:1–4:18

- *Eli and Samuel:* Eli served as a priest and judge in Shiloh. During that time, a woman named Hannah appealed to God for a son and vowed to surrender the child to a life of service to God. Her prayer was answered, and she gave birth to a son—Samuel. She gave Samuel to Eli to be raised in the service of the Lord.

- *Eli's sinful sons:* Eli's own sons, although they were priests, did not truly serve God. They defiled the offerings and lay with the women who served in the tabernacle. Eli mildly rebuked his sons but neglected to take any meaningful action. A prophet told Eli that the Lord would raise up another who would serve him properly. The Lord called Samuel and told him about impending doom for Eli and his sons.

Judges and Prophets

Judges were liberators whom God raised up for special purposes. Prophets were God's witnesses who brought the word of the Lord to the people. Two judges, Deborah and Samuel, were also prophets (Judg. 4:4; 1 Sam. 3:20).

- *Eli's death:* When a battle with the Philistines was going poorly for the Israelites, they brought the ark of the covenant onto the battlefield. Yet the Philistines won the battle anyway. They captured the ark and killed Eli's two sons. When told of the awful news, Eli—who was ninety-eight years old and very heavy—fell backward, broke his neck, and died. He had served Israel for forty years.

14. Samuel – The transitional judge

1 Samuel 1:1–28; 3:1–21; 7:15–17; 10:1; 16:1–13

- *Samuel's leadership:* After Eli's death, Samuel led Israel to repentance, and the Israelites defeated the Philistines. Samuel made his sons judges but they did evil in the sight of the Lord.

- *The people's request:* The Israelites asked that Samuel anoint a king to rule over them. Samuel was displeased but nevertheless brought their request to the Lord. God said that he would give them a king, but warned that the king would take their sons, daughters, fields, servants, and money. The people wanted a king nonetheless.

Samuel
(J. G. Schreiner, c. 1840)

- *The transition from judges to kings:* Samuel anointed a young man named Saul to be the first king of Israel. All went well until King Saul disobeyed God. So God promised to raise up another king, one after his own heart. God led Samuel to anoint a young shepherd named David as the next king. Samuel, the last judge of Israel, died before David took the throne.

CHAPTER 4

Life of Samson

The story of Samson is exciting, and his prowess and strength have become legendary. However, as we read the story carefully, we come to realize that it is not so much about Samson as it is about God. The central question in the story is one that the Israelites of Samson's day had even stopped asking: "Will God rescue us?" Instead of seeking an answer, they were resigned to their fate.

We can see in the book of Judges that Samson often acted on his own for his own selfish purposes. He appeared unaware that God was using all of those decisions to further his plans to rescue his people. Just like the Israelites, Samson often ignored God. But in times of dire need, Samson turned to God in prayer:

Samson (Valentin de Boulogne, 1630–31)

- Samson prayed when he was dying of thirst, and God answered his prayer and gave him water (Judg. 15:18–19).
- Samson prayed when he was captured and humiliated by the Philistines, and God gave him strength one last time (Judg. 16:23–30).

God is always ready and willing to help his people. Even when we forget to pray to God, he is ready to act on our behalf. And when we turn to God in desperation, he will hear our prayers.

ISRAEL AND ITS NEIGHBORS

After going out of Egypt with Moses in the exodus, the Israelites wandered through the wilderness for forty years. As they approached the promised land, leadership moved from Moses to Joshua. The book of Joshua tells us about how the Israelites entered the land and how God gave them victory over their enemies. But God also cautioned them:

> Do not associate with these nations that remain among you; do not invoke the names of their gods or swear by them. You must not serve them or bow down to them.
>
> JOSHUA 23:7

God had promised Abraham to give the land to his descendants (Gen. 12:6–7). In Joshua, God fulfilled his promises.

However, there were still peoples in and around the promised land who did not serve the Lord God: the Canaanites, Moabites, Philistines, Ammonites, and Midianites. These nations were left in the land as a test of Israel's loyalty and trust in God. We read in the book of Judges that God allowed them to remain in the land because "they will become traps for you, and their gods will become snares to you" (Judg. 2:3). The stories in the book of Judges show that the Israelites "did evil in the eyes of the LORD and served the Baals" (Judg. 2:11), and, at the end of the book, "everyone did as they saw fit" (Judg. 21:25).

The arrival of the judges, then, was a desperate and necessary correction. But as the book of Judges shows, instead of improving Israel's spiritual life, things got progressively worse. The time of the judges in Israel was a bad time—a time of uncertainty, insecurity, unfaithfulness, disobedience, oppression, and distance from God. It is in this context that the story of Samson begins.

PEOPLE WITHOUT HOPE

At the outset of Samson's story, we are told that "the Israelites did evil in the eyes of the LORD" (Judg. 13:1). As a consequence, God delivered them into the hands of the Philistines for forty years, an entire generation. It is a long oppression. The other stories of the judges begin when Israel rebels, their enemies oppress them, and then they cry out to God for a liberator. But the story of Samson is different. There is no crying out by Israel; no call for God to rescue them. The people appear resigned to the idea that their situation is not going to change: "Don't you realize that the Philistines are rulers over us?" (Judg. 15:11). Though they seem to have given up hope, God takes the initiative and intervenes miraculously on behalf of his people.

Unlike the other judges' stories, Samson's is the only one with a birth announcement. This divine miracle is further highlighted by the couple chosen: a barren and childless husband and wife. God uses Samson's mother's barren state to display his power, glory, and compassion—as he did with Sarah before her and Hannah and Elizabeth after her. The angel of the Lord appears to her and tells her about the miraculous pregnancy. When she gives birth, she names her son Samson, a name that seems to be connected with the Hebrew word for sun. Samson's name probably means "little sun."

The contrast between Samson's mother and father (Manoah) is interesting. Many Bible scholars believe that they represent the different attitudes of the people of Israel during this time.

SAMSON'S MOTHER	SAMSON'S FATHER
She accepts the word of the angel of the Lord.	He does not believe his wife's words.
She obeys the instructions of the angel of the Lord.	He seems to try to treat the divine visitor like a pagan god. The angel of the Lord rejects his offer and instructs him to offer a sacrifice to God.
She demonstrates wisdom by receiving God's word, obeying it, and realizing that God is doing something amazing on their behalf.	He initially fails to recognize that God is about to do something amazing through him and his wife.

THE NAZIRITE VOW

The angel of God instructed Samson's mother to follow the rules of a Nazirite vow because "the boy will be a Nazirite of God from the womb until the day of his death" (Judg. 13:7). Samson's mother followed the rules of the Nazirite vow until the baby was born.

The word *Nazirite* comes from the Hebrew word *nazir* meaning "consecrated" or "devoted." It refers to a vow that people took to consecrate themselves in a special way to God. The vow could be temporary or permanent. The Bible does not explain why the vow was taken. Some scholars think that it was taken along with specific prayer petitions.

The regulations for the Nazirite vow are found in Numbers 6:1–21, and include:

- abstinence from wine and strong drink;
- refraining from cutting the hair on one's head during the time of the vow; and
- avoidance of contact with the dead.

We have four examples of the Nazirite vow in the Bible:

- Samson (Judg. 13:5)
- John the Baptist (Luke 1:15)
- The apostle Paul (Acts 18:18)
- Samuel (1 Sam. 1:11)

THE PHILISTINES

Samson was chosen by God to "take the lead in delivering Israel from the hand of the Philistines" (Judg. 13:5). The Philistines played an important role in the life of early Israel. In fact, their influence continued well into King David's rule. But who were they? The simple answer is that we are not entirely sure.

Archaeological evidence suggests that they came to the Levant (a region of the Middle East) in a series of migrations from the Aegean (Greece) region. Around the year 1200 BC, the entire region of the Near

East experienced dramatic changes. The powerful kingdoms to the north, the Hittites and the Ugaritians, disappeared for reasons still unclear. To the south, Egypt experienced civil conflict and surprising defeats by a group they called "Sea Peoples." These Sea Peoples seemed to be mercenaries that came from the Canaan region. Scholars think that they were Philistines or related to the Philistines. The migration of these people by sea and land took a long time; Abraham and Isaac—long before Samson—already had some contact with Philistines (Gen. 20:2; 26:1).

By the time of the judges, the Philistines had become part of the land. They had adopted the customs and deities of the area. One of their main gods, Dagon, was an ancient Canaanite god of fertility connected to both grain and fish.

The Philistines were organized in five major cities: Gaza, Ashdod, Ashkelon, Gath, and Ekron. When, at the end of his life, Samson destroyed the temple of Dagon, the five rulers of these cities were present (Judg. 16:23).

View of the Valley of Sorek, looking westward toward Philistia (Photo by Paul Wright)

Samson among the Philistines

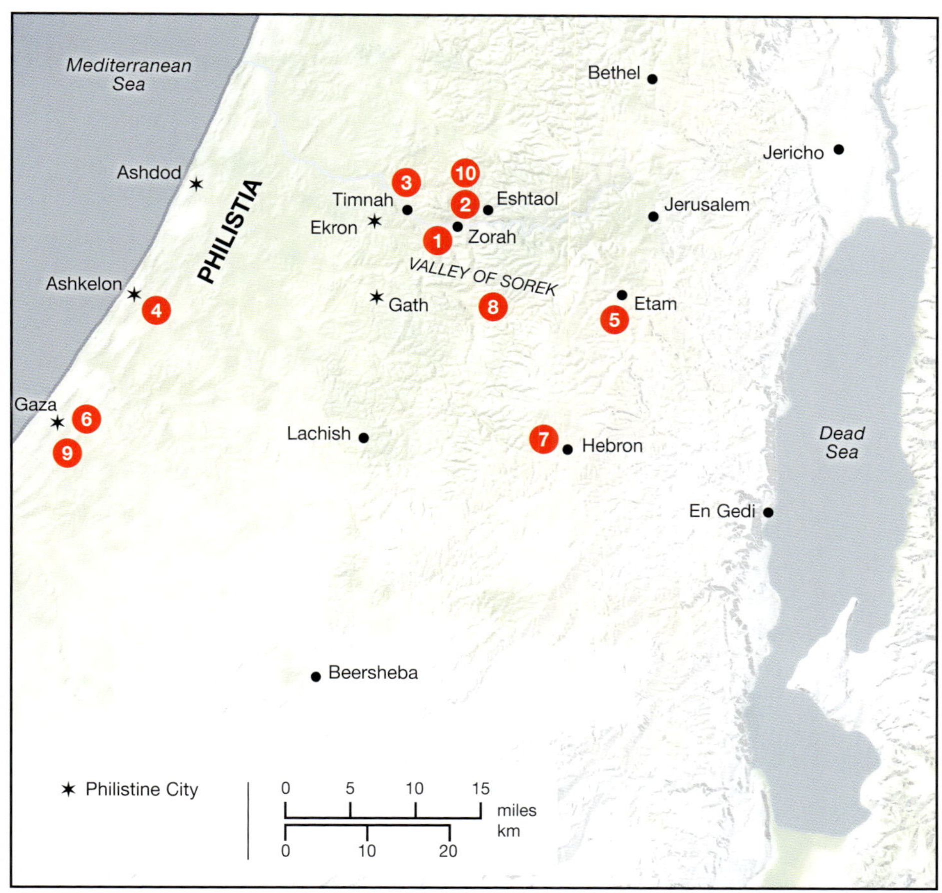

1. Samson is born in Zorah. Judg. 13:2
2. The Spirit of the Lord stirs in Samson between Zorah and Eshtaol. Judg. 13:25
3. Samson marries a Philistine woman in Timnah. Judg. 14:1
4. Samson kills thirty Philistines in Ashkelon. Judg. 14:19
5. Samson hides from the Philistines in Etam. Judg. 15:8
6. Samson visits a prostitute in Gaza. Judg. 16:1
7. Samson carries the gates of Gaza to a hill facing Hebron. Judg. 16:3
8. Samson meets Delilah in the valley of Sorek. Judg. 16:4
9. Samson is taken prisoner and dies with the Philistines in Gaza. Judg. 16:21, 30
10. Samson is buried between Zorah and Eshtaol. Judg. 16:31

TIMELINE

Divine Activity	Event	Samson's Actions
God Intervened	Birth	Samson is born by God's own initiative to an infertile couple (Judg. 13:1–25).
God Moved	Marriage	Samson falls in love with a Philistine woman and marries her. God moved him to do that (Judg. 14:1–4).
God Empowered	Heroic Act	Samson kills a lion with his bare hands. Later, he takes honey from the carcass (Judg. 14:5–6; 8–9).
God Empowered	Heroic Act	Samson kills thirty Philistine men after having been betrayed and losing his bet (Judg. 14:19–20).
God Allowed	Heroic Act	Samson gets revenge against the Philistines for having taken away his wife. With three hundred foxes, he destroys the Philistines' grain fields, "shocks and standing grain, together with vineyards and olive groves" (Judg. 15:1–5).
God Empowered	Heroic Act	Samson flees to Judah, where he is bound and handed over to the Philistines. Samson kills one thousand Philistines using a donkey's jawbone as a weapon (Judg. 15:9–17).
God Provided	Prayer	After his heroic act, Samson thinks he will die of thirst and prays to God. God provides water for him (Judg. 15:18–19).
God Was Silent	Visited a Prostitute	Samson spends the night with a prostitute in the Philistine city of Gaza (Judg. 16:1).
God Was Silent	Heroic Act	Samson tricks the Philistines who were trying to capture him, removes the doors of the city gate, and carries them "to the top of the hill that faces Hebron" (Judg. 16:2–3).
God Was Silent	A Fatal Love	Samson falls in love with another Philistine woman: Delilah (Judg. 16:4).
God Was Silent	Betrayal	After three attempts, Delilah unveils the secret of Samson's strength and betrays him to the Philistines who capture him (Judg. 16:5–22).
God Listened and Empowered	Prayed for Victory	While enslaved and humiliated at his enemies' temple, Samson prays to God to grant him victory over his enemies. God strengthens him for one last time. Samson "killed many more when he died than while he lived" (Judg. 16:23–31).

THE SHOWDOWN

Samson made many mistakes in his life but none so devastating as the trust he put in Delilah. Samson fell in love with Delilah, but she loved money. The Philistines offered her a great sum of money to reveal the secret of Samson's strength.

Though Samson often broke his Nazirite vow, it appears that he did keep one part of the vow: his long hair. The true secret of his strength was that the Spirit of the Lord was with him, but in Samson's eyes, it was his long locks (Judg. 16:17).

Samson fooled Delilah three times by telling her that his strength was in things like bowstrings, ropes, and fabrics. He may have thought that he—the strongest man around—had the advantage, but "pride goes before destruction, a haughty spirit before a fall" (Prov. 16:18). After Delilah's relentless pleading, Samson finally gave in and put his trust not in God who had empowered him, but in Delilah. He revealed to her that no razor had ever touched his head. She quickly betrayed him by having his hair cut while he slept. Samson's super strength was gone.

Samson and the Philistines (Carl Bloch, 1863)

The Philistines captured Samson, blinded him, and took him down to the Philistine city of Gaza. They celebrated their triumph and praised their god, Dagon, saying, "Our god has delivered our enemy into our hands" (Judg. 16:24). But who was the real God in this situation? The

Philistines believed that Dagon delivered Samson into their hands; but it was the Lord God of Israel who gave the Philistines into the hands of Samson.

The Philistines brought their blind prisoner into their temple to mock him. But now, Samson's hair had begun to grow again. He prayed to God to give him strength to "get revenge on the Philistines for my two eyes" (Judg. 16:28). God granted him strength, and Samson reached: "Bracing himself against [the temple pillars], his right hand on the one and his left hand on the other" (Judg. 16:29). His last words were "Let me die with the Philistines!" Samson pushed the pillars, and the temple collapsed on "the rulers and all the people in it" (Judg. 16:30). That day Samson "killed many more when he died than while he lived" (Judg. 16:30).

Samson Destroys the Temple (Joli Antonio, 18th century, Civic Museum of Modena)

STRENGTHS AND WEAKNESSES

On the surface, it would appear that Samson acted selfishly—never for the sake of Israel. Samson was motivated by anger, revenge, and lust. However, God used Samson's own weaknesses to further his plans for Israel. God chose Samson as his agent. We read in his story: "His parents did not know that this was from the LORD" (Judg. 14:4). This Bible verse reminds us that God works behind the scenes, moving the action to free his people from oppression and draw them back to himself.

Samson's weaknesses:

- Lived a life of pleasure seeking.
- Lusted after Philistine women.
- Was moved by his desire to seek revenge.
- Often broke his Nazirite vow.

Samson's acts of strength:

- Killed a lion with his bare hands (Judg. 14:5–6).
- Killed thirty Philistine men after having been betrayed (Judg. 14:19–20).
- Burned grain fields, vineyards, and olive groves with three hundred foxes (Judg. 15:1–5).
- Killed one thousand Philistines using a donkey's jawbone as a weapon (Judg. 15:9–17).
- Removed the doors of the city gate and carried them to the other side of Judah (Judg. 16:2–3).
- Brought down the columns of a Philistine temple and killed many Philistines, including their chief rulers (Judg. 16:23–31).

SAMSON AND ISRAEL

The story of Samson illustrates Israel's unfaithfulness and lack of devotion to God in contrast with God's faithfulness and compassion. It also illustrates a theme common throughout Scripture: Out of despair, God brings hope, and out of suffering, God grants victory.

	SAMSON	ISRAEL
SPECIAL BIRTH	Samson was born by special divine intervention from a woman unable to have children (Judg. 13:1–25).	Israel traced their ancestry to Isaac who was born by special divine intervention from a woman unable to have children (Gen. 17:19–22; 21:1–7).
CONSECRATED TO GOD	Samson was chosen to perform God's mighty acts of salvation from the Philistine oppressors. He should have been a Nazirite for life (Judg. 13:5).	Israel was chosen to become God's people; through Israel, came the promised Messiah–the Savior of the world (Gen. 12:1–3).
REBELLIOUS AND DISLOYAL	Samson was revengeful, pleasure-seeking, foolish, and often broke his Nazirite vow.	Israel rebelled against God by worshiping other gods, denying justice, oppressing the weak, and by becoming unfaithful to God (Ezek. 8:16; Mic. 6:9–16).
CALLED ON GOD IN TIMES OF CRISIS	Samson cried out to God when he almost died of thirst (Judg. 15:18–19) and when he had been humiliated by his enemies at the temple of Dagon (Judg. 16:28).	When Israel's very existence was threatened, the people cried out to God (Ex. 2:24; Judg. 2:18; Ps. 18:6; 107:27–30; 34:17; Jer. 29:12–13; 33:3).
USED BY GOD FOR GOOD	Samson became God's instrument to punish the Philistines and free Israel from their oppression (Judg. 16:30–31).	Israel became a blessing to all the nations, as God has promised (Gen. 12:1–3; Isa. 2:1–5; Gal. 3:7–9).

SAMSON AND JESUS

Samson was at many times a disloyal servant of God. However, God used Samson's personal failings to accomplish his goals. It does not mean that God approved of Samson's rebellion. In fact, Samson's character in the story is a mirror that the author holds in front of God's people. Samson's outright rebellion mirrors ancient Israel's own, revealing the attitudes that God's own people had in contrast with God's own character.

Jesus, although being God, became a humble and obedient servant. In a wonderfully poetical way, the apostle Paul writes this about Jesus:

> Who, being in very nature God, did not consider equality with God something to be used to his own advantage; rather, he made himself nothing by taking the very nature of a servant, being made in human likeness. And being found in appearance as a man, he humbled himself by becoming obedient to death—even death on a cross!
>
> PHILIPPIANS 2:6–8

In contrast with Samson's arrogance and rebellion, Jesus's humility and obedience set the pattern for God's people: "I have set an example that you should do as I have done for you" (John 13:15). Behind Jesus's servant heart was his radical love for his creation.

In conclusion, from Samson's story, we learn that:

- God is loyal to his promises.
- God is full of grace and compassion toward those who suffer.
- God uses for good the weaknesses of his servants.
- Jesus teaches us the meaning of true servanthood.

CHAPTER 5

The Story of Ruth

Life can throw us unexpected and painful surprises. It can change in a single moment: a tragic car accident, an ill-timed jump into a pool, a catastrophic tornado, or a broken relationship that drags us and others through horrible and sad experiences. Even worse, one terrible event might bring about another. As the saying goes, when it rains, it pours. When events overturn our lives, we can get lost in grief and hurt. We might experience a loss of identity and lose sight of the things that make us who we are. It is a time of disorientation.

The Old Testament story of Ruth and Naomi explores the problems of loss and identity. The book of Ruth contains much wisdom for our lives today. The book is a love story. It is a love story between Ruth and Boaz, and also one that illustrates the love between God and his people. It is a story that portrays God and his unfailing love and ceaseless loyalty.

In the story of Ruth, we encounter loss and suffering, disappointment and disorientation, uncertainty and bitterness. But we also find good news; we find love, commitment, perseverance, hope, and God's powerful and tender hand throughout. It is a story about transformation, about God turning our "wailing into dancing" (Ps. 30:11).

The book of Ruth can be viewed as a narrative with four main scenes:

1. A tragic story in a foreign land (Ruth 1:1–22)
2. A new life and a new hope (Ruth 2:1–23)
3. A decisive encounter (Ruth 3:1–18)
4. From emptiness to fullness (Ruth 4:1–15)

SCENE 1: A TRAGIC STORY IN A FOREIGN LAND

"In the days when the judges ruled..." marks the setting for the story (Ruth 1:1). It sends readers back to a time when "Israel had no king; everyone did as they saw fit" (Judg. 21:25). Israel's social and spiritual life was a mess. The time of the judges was known for its cycle of disobedience, repentance, God's intervention, gratitude, and back again to disobedience. Although the text does not say that the famine was a punishment from God, the mention of the days of the judges makes this connection possible.

Whatever the case, we find a man from Bethlehem (the name Bethlehem means "house of bread") leaving town and heading to the foreign land of Moab because of a famine. Already we know that things are not the way they are supposed to be—the "house of bread" is running out of bread.

The names of the man and his family increase the likelihood that we are in for a surprising story. The man's name, Elimelek, most likely means "my God is king." In those times, one of the main functions of a king was to provide security and food for his people. A good king made sure his people did not suffer hunger. Moreover, the names of Elimelek's sons suggest that the story will take a tragic turn. Mahlon means something equivalent to "sickly" and Kilion "weakly." With those names, we suspect that they will not be in the story for too long. Elimelek's wife's name seems to be the only good news: Naomi's name means "pleasant." But in a story that promises surprises, we can anticipate a great surprise for Naomi as well.

A threshing floor located east of Bethlehem (Photo by Paul Wright)

In three short verses, we read that Elimelek died and, after ten years, so did Mahlon and Kilion. "Naomi was left without her two sons and her husband" (Ruth 1:5). Before moving on in the story, let's pause to fully appreciate the full effect of those words. In the cultural world during the time of the Old Testament, women were valued only by their connection to a man, typically a father or husband. A woman's security and safety depended on her father's, husband's, or sons' ability to provide for her. When a woman lost her husband, as Naomi did, her value declined steeply, and her safety and security then depended on her sons. When Naomi lost her sons too, she became destitute. Now she was on a social level below servants, and making matters worse, she was a foreigner in Moab. The turn of fortunes for Naomi is total and paralyzing. Her life is overturned. As Naomi exclaims, "The Lord has turned against me!" (Ruth 1:13).

Naomi is not the only one in a bad situation. Her daughters-in-law, Ruth and Orpah, are in a similar predicament. They are also widows. Although the biblical text never states it, Ruth and Orpah do not (or cannot) have children. Ten years of marriage to Naomi's sons did not produce children for either woman. By cultural tradition, both women were attached to Naomi, their mother-in-law, to share her fate. Naomi, however, graciously releases them from their cultural duty and encourages them to go back to their mothers, to at least have the possibility of a future. After some argument, Orpah decides to go back. Ruth, however,

Naomi and Ruth

decides to stay with her mother-in-law. It is a courageous decision, and one that comes from a deep love, commitment, and loyalty to Naomi. Naomi calls this love *hesed* ("kindness;" Ruth 1:8). This is a Hebrew word that is most often used to describe God's love, commitment, and loyalty toward Israel.

> Don't urge me to leave you or to turn back from you. Where you go I will go, and where you stay I will stay. Your people will be my people and your God my God. Where you die I will die, and there I will be buried. May the LORD deal with me, be it ever so severely, if even death separates you and me.
>
> RUTH 1:16–17

Ruth leaves her home, her identity, and her possibility of a favorable future, and joins Naomi in what could only be a future filled with more suffering. Yet her actions are just what Naomi needs. Naomi leaves Moab, and when she is back in Bethlehem she says, "I went away full, but the LORD has brought me back empty. Why call me Naomi? The LORD has afflicted me; the Almighty has brought misfortune upon me" (Ruth 1:21). Naomi changes her name; she is now Mara, which means "bitter" (Ruth 1:20).

Returning to Bethlehem must have been a very difficult decision for Naomi. All that she had died in Moab. But she heard that "the LORD had come to the aid of his people by providing food for them" in Bethlehem (Ruth 1:6). Naomi understood that life for her back in her village of Bethlehem would be better. God commanded the Israelites to protect the weakest people in the community:

> Do not deprive the foreigner or the fatherless of justice, or take the cloak of the widow as a pledge. Remember that you were slaves in Egypt and the LORD your God redeemed you from there. That is why I command you to do this.
>
> DEUTERONOMY 24:17–18

> Learn to do right; seek justice. Defend the oppressed. Take up the cause of the fatherless; plead the case of the widow.
>
> ISAIAH 1:17

The second chapter of Ruth opens with a hopeful reminder: "Naomi had a relative on her husband's side, a man of standing … whose name was Boaz" (Ruth 2:1).

For Ruth, life in Bethlehem would certainly not be easy. She is female, a foreigner, barren, and widowed. Yet her commitment was firm and exemplary. She took it upon herself to care for her sorrowful mother-in-law. "As it turned out" (Ruth 2:3), the text tells us, Ruth just happened to be gathering her grain in a plot of land that belonged to Boaz.

Names in the Book of Ruth

NAME	MEANING	SIGNIFICANCE
Naomi	"Pleasant"	Early in the story, her life is quite unpleasant. So Naomi changes her name to Mara, which means "bitter."
Elimelek	"My God is king"	Kings in the ancient world were supposed to provide for the needs of their people, including food and security. Yet, a great famine forces a family into exile.
Bethlehem	"House of bread"	Elimelek and his family leave Bethlehem during a famine to find bread in Moab, Israel's hated enemy.
Mahlon and Kilion	Something like "sickly" and "weakly"	Their names suggest that the two brothers will have a tragic end.
Ruth	Related to the idea of "refreshment," or maybe "friendship"	Although a Moabite, Ruth becomes a friend of God's people, and a refreshment to her mother-in-law, Naomi.
Boaz	Though difficult to determine, some possible meanings include "lively," "strength," and "by strength" or "with strength."	Boaz surely demonstrates great strength of character and convictions to carry another person's–Naomi's closer relative's–responsibility toward Naomi.

Journey of Naomi and Her Family

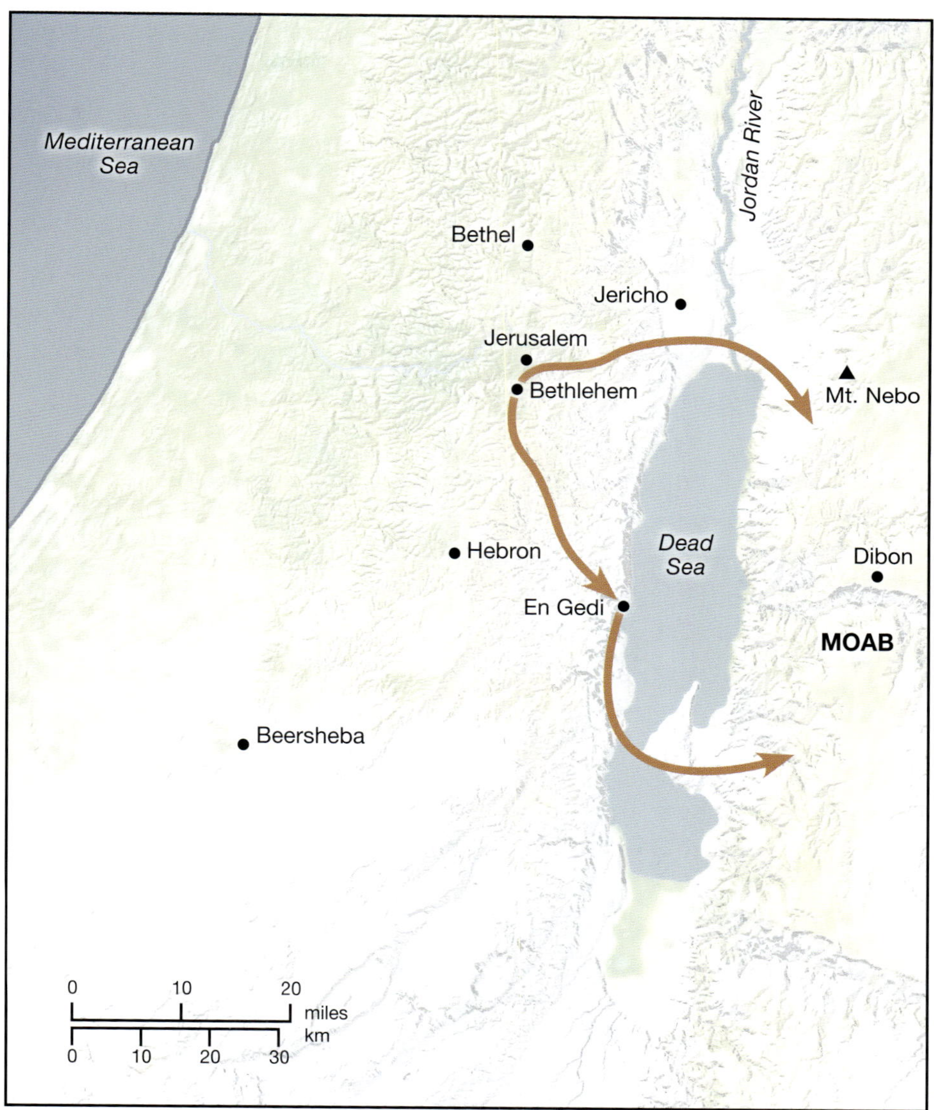

The exact route taken by Elimelek, Naomi, and their sons is unknown, but the map shown here provides two probable options: First, a northern route would have taken them across the Jordan River through the plains of Moab, a similar route (but in reverse) to the one Joshua traversed many years earlier to enter Canaan. Second, a southern route would have taken them across the shallow part of the Dead Sea.

SCENE 2: A NEW LIFE AND A NEW HOPE

These three Hebrew words, *ish gibbor hayil*, are used to describe Boaz in Ruth 2:1. Translated sometimes as "a man of standing" or "a worthy man," these words offer clues to the character of Boaz. The first part of the expression, *ish gibbor*, means "man mighty in," and *hayil* can indicate strength, power, ability, honor, or wealth. In his social context, Boaz is a man well respected and known for his character and leadership. Socially, Boaz stands galaxies away from Ruth's social status.

We also learn about Boaz's spiritual character when he arrives at his field and greets his servants. Boaz is a pious and well-liked person; his servants' love for him suggests that he is a fair and honest person. He is so in touch with his servants that he even notices a new person following his harvesters. He approaches Ruth and makes an offering that speaks volumes about his character. Boaz greets his servants with, "The LORD be with you!" (Ruth 2:4). Indeed, the Lord's presence becomes evident in Boaz's own righteous and compassionate character toward his servants and Ruth. Boaz makes offers to Ruth worthy of his character:

- Permission to stay and gather grain in his field
- Permission to be with his servants
- Protection from the men in the field
- Provision to share in the water of his workers

Although the first offer fulfills the command to provide for the poor (Lev. 19:9; 23:22; Deut. 24:19), Boaz went far beyond the requirements of the law. Ruth's social condition places her below even the poor Israelites following the harvesters. Not only that, but providing his protection to her from the men reminds us that women then, as often is the case today, can be targets for abuse and violence. However, Boaz offered more than protection; he made Ruth, for all practical purposes, part of his household. Again, Ruth was socially far below Boaz's servants, but now she shares in their water. Further, Boaz invites Ruth to his own table to share his bread. It is more than a generous gesture; it is a righteous and compassionate deed.

Boaz is not finished showcasing his character. Unknown to Ruth, he orders his servants to leave extra grain, and even stalks of wheat, for Ruth to pick up. Ruth ends up with about thirty pounds of grain to take home. According to documents from Babylon around that time, harvesters would take home one or two pounds a day. Ruth took home more than ten times the salary of a harvester. In addition, she took home left-over cooked grain for Naomi. While the great amount of grain Ruth brought back home was impressive, for a hungry Naomi the sight of already cooked grain was a blessing beyond words. Ruth's care and commitment soothed Naomi's bitterness and grief.

Ruth and Boaz (Eduard Holbein, 1830)

Why did Boaz act in such a way toward Ruth? The answer, in part, is that he acted from his own commitment and character. The answer is also found in his own words. Ruth bows down with her face to the ground (as a person in her social standing would be expected to) and asks, "Why have I found such favor in your eyes that you notice me—a foreigner?" (Ruth 2:10). Boaz answers, "I've been told all about what you have done for your mother-in-law since the death of your husband" (Ruth 2:11). Boaz is moved to compassion because of Ruth's own loyalty and commitment to Naomi. Ruth's love and commitment exemplify the attitude that God's people should have toward those in need. Ruth's unrelenting and selfless love toward Naomi enraptured Boaz.

In the times of the Bible, marriage was more an economic than a romantic affair. Boaz had nothing to gain from courting a foreign woman from the lowest rung of the social ladder. And that is exactly what makes Boaz's actions even more extraordinary—a man doing what is right without expecting anything in return. Boaz's loving actions were a response to Ruth's own loving commitment and loyalty to Naomi. Although not at the same social level, Ruth is his match on a spiritual level.

Hesed

Most of the time in the Old Testament, the word *hesed* is used in connection to a covenant, as it is in the book of Ruth (Ruth 1:8; 2:20; 3:10). This word implies that people are not only willing to fulfill their covenant obligations but also to go beyond them for the sake of an important relationship. *Hesed*, then, suggests taking loyalty, commitment, compassion, and love a step beyond what is required.

With great joy, Naomi receives Ruth's gifts through Boaz and cries out, "Blessed be the man who took notice of you!" (Ruth 2:19). Naomi had bitterly complained that God's noticing her had brought much affliction (Ruth 1:21). When she learns that the man's name is Boaz, a light comes on in her mind: "He has not stopped showing his kindness [*hesed*] to the living and the dead" (Ruth 2:20). Who is the "he" referring to? Boaz or the Lord? It is not clear, though it probably refers to both. In Boaz's *hesed* Naomi recognizes the Lord's *hesed*.

After so much heartbreak and bitterness, Naomi finds comfort through the loving and compassionate acts of Ruth and Boaz. Although the text does not say it this way, we can recognize that God has reached out and touched Naomi through Ruth and Boaz. We would expect God to use his people this way. Boaz, after all, is an Israelite of impeccable character and reputation. But Ruth … well, notice the way Ruth is introduced in this chapter: "Ruth the Moabite" and "the Moabite who came back from Moab" (Ruth 2:2, 6). She is a Moabite, one of Israel's most ferocious enemies, and is seen as a pagan (remember that Naomi asked her to return to her gods and her family; Ruth 1:15). Boaz behaves the way all Israelites should. Ruth, although not from Israel, also behaves as an Israelite should.

SCENE 3: A DECISIVE ENCOUNTER

As she realizes that God is blessing her, Naomi's grief is diminished. But Naomi is still empty, and Ruth's future is still precarious. They are still poor, widowed, childless, and, in Ruth's case, a foreigner. With renewed hope, Naomi reciprocates Ruth's kindness with a plan of her own. What will happen to Ruth if Naomi dies? Her prospects are even grimmer without her mother-in-law. Having witnessed the righteous character of her relative Boaz, Naomi makes a rather risky plan. Ruth is to approach Boaz in the middle of the night, after a time of celebration following the harvest, while he sleeps outside the city, where the threshing floor was most likely located. With any other man, such a plan would be a recipe for disaster. However, relying on Boaz's righteous character, Naomi is sure that Ruth will be safe.

Naomi explains her plan to Ruth and concludes, "He will tell you what to do" (Ruth 3:4). Ruth replies, "I will do whatever you say" (Ruth 3:5). With this plan, Naomi is showing her *hesed* to Ruth. Naomi is seeking a husband for Ruth; a husband like Boaz would assure a future for Ruth. Naomi is taking a risk with her own future too. Once married, Ruth and the land of Naomi's late husband would belong to Boaz. Naomi could end up with nothing; she could be completely destitute. Yet, Naomi knows Ruth's character and trusts her. Now more than ever, Naomi's future is tied to Ruth's. Filled with risks, this plan depends on Ruth's kindness and, as it turns out, also Boaz's.

Interestingly, Ruth does not follow Naomi's instructions entirely. She, instead, tells Boaz what to do. After waking up Boaz, she says, "Spread the corner of your garment over me, since you are a guardian-redeemer of our family" (Ruth 3:9). Boaz does not react in anger to Ruth's daring actions. He replies, "The Lord bless you, my daughter. This kindness [*hesed*] is greater than that which you showed earlier" (Ruth 3:10). It is not completely clear what Boaz is referring to by the earlier kindness. But something Ruth has done has made a great impression on Boaz.

In the Hebrew Bible, the book of Ruth follows the book of Proverbs. By being there, the book of Ruth connects the character of Ruth with the last poem in Proverbs: The Wife of Noble Character (Prov. 31:10–31). The poem in Proverbs begins with the words *eshet hayil*: "A wife [or woman] of noble character who can find?" (verse 10). The answer is Ruth. She is the *eshet hayil*, the woman of noble character (Ruth 3:11).

Ruth's request to "spread the corner of your garment" is a phrase used elsewhere in the Old Testament. In Ezekiel, the prophet uses the image of marriage to illustrate God's relationship with Israel. The prophet employs the same expression, "I spread the corner of my garment over you" (Ezek. 16:8), as a symbolic gesture for the marriage covenant. Ruth is asking Boaz to marry her—a very daring request from a woman to a man. However, the words Ruth uses reflect Boaz's own words back in his field in Ruth 2:12: "… under whose [God's] wings you have come to take refuge." (The words *wing* and *corner* are the same word in Hebrew.) Being covered by Boaz's garment represents God's own covering of Ruth. She not only requests Boaz to marry her, but she goes beyond her own needs and future and requests that Boaz also redeem (buy back) Elimelek's land for Naomi, which would then provide a secure future for Naomi. Ruth's ability to think beyond herself and consider her mother-in-law's needs shows her commitment to Naomi.

Ruth's requests to Boaz include two important social protections in the law: the levirate marriage and the guardian-redeemer. These two ancient practices had a very practical social and theological purpose: to assure both the safety of descendants and the possession of ancestral family land. Ancient Israelites derived much of their identity as God's people from these two social realities. Sons were to carry the family name and the land, which was the concrete expression of God's promises to Abraham. To this point, Ruth's explicit identity has been that of a foreign woman who accompanies her Israelite widowed mother-in-law. To the reader, it has become increasingly clear that Ruth behaves just as an Israelite

When an Israelite man experienced hard times, his nearest relative was required to help him. This nearest relative, the guardian-redeemer (also called kinsman-redeemer), would buy the land of the needy man to prevent it from becoming the possession of someone outside the clan (Lev. 25:25).

A levirate marriage was a provision in the Mosaic law that guaranteed that the lineage of a man who died without a son would continue. The nearest relative would marry the widow of the man so she could bear sons (Deut. 25:5–10). Additionally, this law provided protection for a widow who could be in danger of becoming indigent in a patriarchal society.

should. In chapter 3, it is also clear that Boaz shares that view, since he has praised her *hesed* twice now. Furthermore, it has become clear to others in the city that Ruth is more than a foreigner: "All the people of my town know that you are a woman of noble character" (Ruth 3:11). "Noble character" translates from a Hebrew expression that connects Ruth with Boaz: *eshet hayil*. Boaz was first introduced in the book as an *ish gibbor hayil*. Once again, the text presents Ruth at the same spiritual level as Boaz, an extraordinary claim in a male dominated world.

Although Boaz promises to do as Ruth has requested, he informs her that a closer relative has the rights of the guardian-redeemer. However, Boaz assures Ruth that if the relative is not willing to exercise his rights, Boaz will do it. As a visible assurance of his promise to Ruth, Boaz gives her "six measures of barley" to fill her shawl (Ruth 3:15). Symbolically, Ruth and Naomi had come to Bethlehem with empty hands, but now Ruth's hands are full. Naomi responds with caution and wisdom: "Wait, my daughter, until you find out what happens" (Ruth 3:18).

SCENE 4: FROM EMPTINESS TO FULLNESS

After the private conversation that Ruth initiated, the scene moves again to the public sphere. In the public sphere, Ruth and Naomi are voiceless and powerless. Boaz becomes their voice. He is a man of strength, of noble character, of great standing in the community. Rather than bullying others to get his way or using his own social capital to accomplish his plans, Boaz acts with wisdom.

Although not explicitly affirmed in the text, God's presence throughout the story is apparent. When Boaz goes up to the town gate, the closer relative (or guardian-redeemer) just happens to come along. God is working behind the scenes, so this turn of events is not merely luck.

While the names of the main characters are important in the story, this relative remains unnamed. This nameless Israelite is willing to redeem the land that belonged to Elimelek, Kilion, and Mahlon, possibly because of the financial benefits that come with it. Boaz quickly reminds him, "On the day you buy the land from Naomi, you also acquire Ruth the Moabite, the dead man's widow" (Ruth 4:5). Notice how Boaz presents Ruth. To this point, Boaz has spoken of Ruth with much admiration and praise: her demonstration of love toward Naomi is noteworthy, and she is described as a woman of noble character, one who any Israelite male would be blessed to marry. But here, Boaz introduces her as "the Moabite," a foreigner who belongs to one of Israel's most hated enemy kingdoms, and "the dead man's widow." Presented this way, Ruth is not a desirable partner but a financial liability. The nameless relative relinquishes his right to redeem Naomi's land. Although not doing anything illegal or immoral, this relative fails to do *hesed* for Naomi's family. Although obeying the law, he is not willing to walk the extra mile.

By means of what seems to have been a formalized ritual, the relative transfers all rights to Boaz. This transfer was made official with an offering of clothing. Here, at the city gate, the piece of clothing is a sandal. This symbolic act formalizes the transaction, and the elders witness it ("We are witnesses;" Ruth 4:11) and bless the foreign woman: "May the Lord make the woman who is coming into your home like Rachel and Leah" (Ruth 4:11). The elders praise Ruth at the gate, just as Proverbs echoes, "Honor her for all that her hands have done, and let her works bring her praise at the city gate" (Prov. 31:31).

Removing one's sandal was a symbolic act that signaled a change of status. When people in the Old Testament express pain, they tear their clothing and put on rough clothing (sackcloth) to symbolize their low emotional state. In the ancient world, when women became widows, such as Naomi and Ruth, they would wear clothing that reflected their new social status. Notice how Ruth, before going to see Boaz, changed her clothing to indicate her new status as one who is open to marriage (Ruth 3:3). Boaz subsequently covers Ruth as a symbol for marriage (Ruth 3:9).

Boaz marries Ruth, and "the Lord enabled her to conceive, and she gave birth to a son" (Ruth 4:13). This is a story of redemption. God could have done mighty wonders with Naomi and Ruth: he could have come in an awesome storm and talked to them, as he did with Job; he could have sent a powerful prophet, as he did with the widow of Zarephath. But he did not. Instead, quietly behind the scenes, God allowed his people to represent him. Boaz's love represents God's own love. Boaz's courageous, compassionate, and righteous actions represent God. Ruth's own courageous, loving, daring, and loyal actions, along with her commitment to Naomi's God, show a way to go beyond the written law and seek the kingdom of God and its righteousness (Matt. 6:33). Ruth, therefore, becomes a model for what *hesed* looks like—not just for women, but for all of God's people.

Genealogy of David

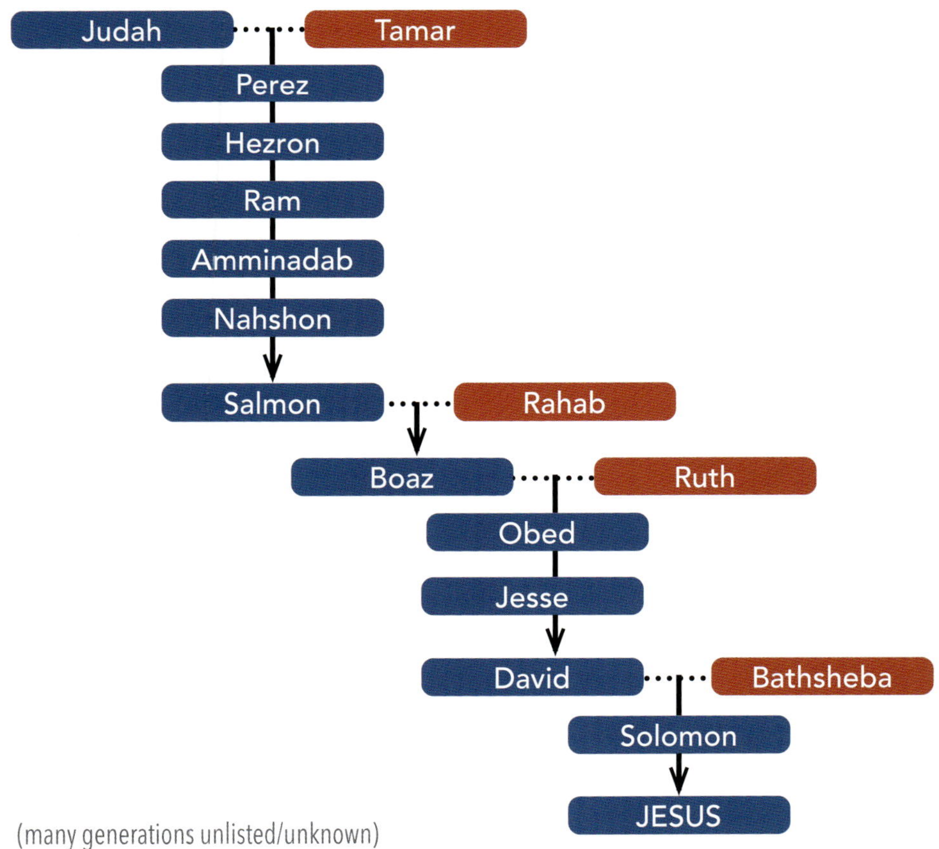

Naomi is no longer "Mara." She is no longer bitter or empty. Now, "Naomi has a son!" (Ruth 4:17). Naomi's identity has been radically changed. Ruth's identity is equally changed. She is no longer a foreign widow. She is now married to a man of noble character; she is a mother; and she is compared to great women of Israel: Rachel, Leah, and Tamar (Ruth 4:12). Ruth is now an Israelite woman, the mother of Obed, the ancestor of the great King David, and, eventually, of the Messiah Jesus (Matt. 1:5–16). God's love—his *hesed*—transforms and renews people!

GOD'S *HESED*

"This is how God showed his love among us: He sent his one and only Son into the world that we might live through him" (1 John 4:9). God's love is so much more than a feeling or an emotion—it is an action. The letter of John teaches us as much. We know about God's immense love in that he sent his own Son to give us life. That is the main quality of *hesed*. It is action that is born from commitment, loyalty, and compassion. If Ruth, Boaz, and Naomi illustrate it for us, Jesus Christ perfects it with his obedience and sacrifice. God's love in Christ gives us new life, makes us a new creation, and enables us to imitate Ruth, Boaz, Naomi, and, especially, Jesus. May our *hesed* be like that of Ruth, Boaz, Naomi, and Jesus!

> We love because he first loved us. Whoever claims to love God yet hates a brother or sister is a liar. For whoever does not love their brother and sister, whom they have seen, cannot love God, whom they have not seen. And he has given us this command: Anyone who loves God must also love their brother and sister.
>
> 1 JOHN 4:19–21

CHAPTER 6

The World of Ancient Israel

The authors of the Bible did not write with the goal of giving us, their readers, a complete account of their own cultural world, but rather to reveal the redemptive hand of God in the daily lives of people. As the Bible's authors received and responded to God's revelation, they were careful to make sure that what God prompted them to communicate was done in ways that their contemporaries could understand. Their messages were couched in expressions, words, and pictures that were part of their own cultural world. This, however, does not mean that the Bible is foreign and outdated to us today. Quite the opposite. Even though the details of our cultural worlds differ, the human condition remains unchanged. By taking the stories and statements of the Bible seriously and reading them in light of the world in which the characters and the writers of the Bible lived, we are able to see ourselves and see how God continues his work within our cultural world. Indeed, a grasp of the cultural world of the Bible is one of the most powerful commentaries on the text of the Bible.

Core elements of Israel's culture were deeply engrained in the behavior of the patriarchs, whom we read about in Genesis. The books of Joshua, Judges, and Ruth cover the time (nearly five hundred years later) when Israel emerged as a cohesive people group in their homeland, which up to that point had been known as Canaan. Ancient Israel's core values, norms, behaviors, and beliefs, not to mention the mundane practicalities of living off their land, all took shape in these early years. This formative period set the

What Is Culture?

Culture is the shared way of life of a group of people. It includes both behavior and artifacts:

- Behavior is what a group thinks, says, values, and does.
- Artifacts are what the group uses in the natural environment where they live.

Culture is learned, shared, and passed on from generation to generation, with changes coming either rapidly or slowly, depending on how closely a culture interacts with a more dominant culture nearby. In short, culture is a group identifier.

tone for the later cultural development that we see in the rest of the Old Testament.

As we read the narratives in Joshua, Judges, and Ruth, we are faced with this question: How was Israelite culture *unique* in the ancient world, and how much of its culture did Israel *share* with its neighbors—for better or worse? As we reflect on this question, it is helpful to remember the apostle Paul's charge: Though we live *in* the world, we are to be transformed by the grace and power of God to live in faithful, helpful, and hopeful ways that *transcend* it (Rom. 12:2). This challenge was as real for the ancient Israelites as it is for us today.

A SHARED LAND

Like all cultures, that of Israel in the days of Joshua and the judges was a mixed bag, partly their own and partly borrowed from people with whom they came into contact. The land of Israel had the same climate, plants, animals, terrain, and natural resources as that of their neighbors. They all struggled with tough living conditions and faced the same challenges to just survive. This shared geography led to ways of living in the land that worked more or less effectively for everyone. There were similarities, not only in activities like raising animals and growing crops, but also in the ways that the Israelites and their neighbors related to each other and even, to an extent, to God (or, in the case of the Canaanites, to their gods).

Sunrise over the Sea of Galilee

But even though the Israelites and their neighbors lived in a shared natural world, the Bible is clear that there were some significant differences between them. Chief among these is the Israelite recognition that there is only one God, that he is the creator of (rather than part of) the natural world, and that he desires to communicate with people in helpful, redemptive ways.

As the Israelites adapted to the living conditions in Canaan, their culture began to be shaped by God's revelation on Mount Sinai through the laws—or the instructions—of Torah ("instruction" is the root meaning of the Hebrew word *Torah*). It was a long, halting, and only somewhat successful process. Ideally, the instructions of Torah were to impact Israel's daily, social, and national life. This involved distinctive behavior in day-to-day living:

- Do not eat pork or fish without scales (Deut. 14:8–10).
- Do not boil a young goat in its mother's milk (Deut. 14:21; which is usually interpreted as not eating milk and meat in the same meal).
- Do not cut the hair at the sides of your head (Lev. 19:27).
- Make sure that the tassel of your garment has a blue thread in it (Num. 15:38; Canaanite garments had tassels, apparently without blue).

- Treat strangers living in your midst as one of your own (Lev. 19:33–34).
- Allow for kinder, gentler forms of punishment for wrongdoing (Num. 35:9–15).

There are a host of others. Some have been adopted into our societies, while others seem eccentric or bizarre, to put it mildly. Yet when seen in light of what was otherwise a common behavior, diet, and dress across the region, all made perfect sense as cultural signs setting Israel apart from their neighbors.

As we read the Bible, it is also helpful to keep in mind that its stories teach by example. Some tell of people endeavoring to follow Torah in the challenges of daily life, while others are blatantly the opposite. Indeed, some of the most jarring actions in Bible stories are not at all typical of ancient Israel's culture but quite the opposite—horrible examples of what was *not* culturally acceptable in their day, or in ours.

Clues from Archaeology

We can learn a great deal about the social, economic, and religious world of ancient Israel and their neighbors by looking at written documents of the time.

- Eighteen clay tablets found at Hazor, a large city in the north conquered by Joshua, mention specific economic transactions, legal cases, acts of divination, and other daily activities connected to Canaanite life in the city.
- Archaeologists have found a broken piece of pottery from the time of the Judges at Izbet Sartah, a small village a few miles from Jerusalem. It is inscribed only with several attempts to write the alphabet, so it seems to have been an early Israelite school exercise.
- Longer texts from Ugarit, an ancient city on the coast north of Canaan, reveal details about the religious worldview of the Canaanites.
- Contemporary texts from Egypt, Israel's closest big neighbor, and Mesopotamia, a bit further away, offer additional information about living conditions in Canaan.

In addition, a wide range of archaeological objects—from plowshares and plant seeds to drinking vessels, houses, and religious objects—offer tangible examples of the material world of the Bible. However, it is seldom possible to say that any given object was used by an Israelite rather than a Canaanite, and vice versa. We wish we had more information, and so we need to proceed cautiously when drawing conclusions from limited and scattered archaeological evidence.

ISRAEL'S NEIGHBORS

If asked, *Who is your neighbor?*, an early Israelite could point to any number of people or groups outside the immediate family, people related distantly by blood. But if we expand the question to the ethnic or national level, the neighbors of ancient Israel were foreigners, most of whom were starting to form nations that bordered Israel at more or less at the same time that Israel was going through the same process.

To the east, in the fertile lands across the Jordan River and the Dead Sea, were the Ammonites, Moabites, and Edomites, anciently related to Israel by blood and cultural connections (Gen. 19:36–38; 36:1). The opening scene of Ruth, for instance, shows us how seamlessly Judeans could move to and live in Moab, marrying Moabites and going about life essentially the same way they had back home. The Israelite tribes of Reuben and Gad settled on land adjacent to Ammonite and Moabite territory east of the Jordan River (the Transjordan), a land better suited their free-range herding ways than the terrain of Canaan (Num. 32:1–5, 33). Given these natural cultural connections, both Moses and Joshua sensed the danger that their descendants would assimilate into Moabite and Ammonite culture, forsaking loyalty to the Lord God in the process (Num. 32:6–15; Josh. 22:1–34).

To the southwest, on the fertile plain edging the Mediterranean Sea, were the Philistines. These were the newcomers, complete foreigners who arrived in waves from the Aegean Sea, speaking a language totally unrelated to that of Israel and bringing a different way of life. We should say "almost different," for all the peoples of the greater Mediterranean world were familiar with what it took to grow grains, grapes, and olives, and to herd sheep and goats—staples of the land. Still, the Philistines were the most different of Israel's neighbors—and they settled in areas that Joshua had assigned to the tribes of Judah and Dan. The stories of Samson and David portray the Philistines as technologically advanced, formidable, and in some cases even attractive to the Israelites. Yet overall, they were feared and treated as people from foreign cultures often are (Judg. 14:1–3; 1 Sam. 13:19–21; 17:4–7).

Canaanite was the umbrella term for people already living within the borders of what was becoming the land of Israel (Num. 34:1–12). *Amorite* was the general term for indigenous people living both east of the Jordan River and in the hilly parts of Canaan (Gen. 48:22; Deut. 1:44; Josh. 10:5). The Bible often uses these terms interchangeably. It also mentions several smaller groups living at various places within the borders of Canaan: the Hittites, Girgashites, Perizzites, Hivites, and Jebusites (Deut. 7:1; Josh 3:10). There must have been others whom we will never know about. These were Israel's next-door neighbors.

The Phoenicians were already well-entrenched along the Mediterranean coast to the northwest. Although they lived outside the borders of Canaan proper, they were culturally Canaanite and preserved elements of Canaanite religion during the centuries when adherence to the Lord God of Israel became dominant in Canaan.

Canaanites tended to be urban dwellers, with their cities surrounded by villages that bolstered their local economies. Everything we know from archaeology portrays them as having advanced technology, sophisticated cultural institutions, and economies connected to international markets. Politically, they operated as mostly independent city-states, yet all had ties to Egypt, their closest super-neighbor. The Israelites settled first in areas between the Canaanite urban centers, and many of them must have had frequent encounters with these, their closest neighbors. Temptations to be like the Canaanites, to bend to the dominant culture, were strong at every level. Like the Canaanites, the daily rhythm of Israelite life was repetitious, closely tied to activities that provided for daily life, fostering tight social connections, trying to become as secure as conditions allowed, and just staying alive. While the Bible focuses on the religious difference between the Canaanites and Israelites, it is also easy to see the never ending, raw struggle for economic and political supremacy in what remained a shared land.

Israel's Neighbors

TRIBAL SOCIETY

Ancient Israel was a tribal society, grounded in relationships defined by blood. Two basic resources were paramount: one's family and one's land. Each person's existence—their roots to the past and their hope for the future—was inextricably tied to an unbroken chain of ancestors and descendants living on ancestral land. An Israelite's connection to land was immediate, necessary, and constant: people were conceived on the ground, ate, slept, and lived on the ground, died, and were buried in the ground. Ideally, all of this took place on their own ancestral plot. The worst thing to happen to someone was not death (that happened to everyone); rather, it was to be forced to live, die, and be buried somewhere other than on their own land (2 Sam. 21:12–14; Josh. 24:29–33).

At the same time, the Israelites were aware that they lived under the ultimate care and protection of God, who is described as their *Father* (*av*), a family term (Deut. 32:6; Ps. 89:26; 103:13). God met people where they were, in specific places, often at home or on their own land (Gen. 18:1; 32:30; Judg. 6:11; 13:2–3). This made the ground holy, personal, something to hold on to, *theirs*.

In all, life was relational rather than task oriented, with wealth counted in honor gained through having a large family, prosperous land, and living rightly (according to the Torah), being at peace with oneself, one's peers, and God.

Modern zodiac with symbols of the twelve tribes (Old City Jerusalem)

There were five main characteristics that shaped an Israelite family:

- It was endogamous. This means that marriages took place between close blood relatives in order to bring together two family units who were willing to strengthen, provide for, and protect each other over an extended period of time. Great value was placed on marrying someone who was already known and trusted, and on keeping resources within the extended family. In the book of Ruth, Elimelek and Naomi's sons push the boundaries by marrying Moabite women (Ruth 1:1–5; 4:3–6). Samson broke cultural norms completely by insisting on marrying a Philistine woman (Judg. 14:1–3).
- It was patrilocal. This means that a bride went to live with her husband's family, not the other way around. Samson's Philistine wife, at the behest of her family, apparently refused to do so, breaking the marriage in the process (Judg. 14:20–15:1).
- It was patrilineal. This means that lineage and inheritance were based on the father's family line and children belonged to the husband's, rather than the wife's, family. Joshua divided the land of Canaan so that each of the tribes of Israel, named after the sons (or grandsons) of Jacob, could receive their own inheritance (Josh. 14:1; 18:2). Boaz married Ruth so that their children could restore the inheritance of land and the family line of Mahlon, Ruth's deceased husband (Ruth 4:9–10).
- It was patriarchal. The oldest man was head of the family, although the oldest woman, the matriarch, also held significant authority in day-to-day affairs. Individuals were typically identified through their fathers, for example, "Joshua son of Nun" (Josh. 2:1) and "Achan son of Karmi" (Josh. 7:1); and wives through their husbands, for example, "Deborah, a prophet, the wife of Lappidoth" (Judg. 4:4) and "Jael, the wife of Heber" (Judg. 4:17).
- It could be polygamous. Men often had more than one wife so a family could have many children. Within that culture, the explanation was the need for large families, the basic support

group of society. This could also serve as a way to bring into a family unit women who might otherwise remain outside formal social structures. Nevertheless, the examples of polygamy in the Bible show that it never brought peace to a family and that monogamy was still the ideal (Gen. 16:1–7; 30:1; 1 Sam. 1:4–8; Deut. 17:17; 21:15–17). Gideon, for instance, had many wives and dozens of sons, but this arrangement ended violently, with seventy of his sons meeting a gruesome death when one son vied for dominance over the others (Judg. 8:30–9:5).

Israel's tribal society was built on a series of groups, or households, each larger than the next. The basic unit of society was not the individual but the *bet 'av*, "father's house" (Judg. 6:15; 9:5; 11:2; 1 Sam. 9:1). Each father's house was an economically self-sufficient, multi-generational family unit headed by a patriarch, with everyone living together in a single housing compound.

Next was the extended family or clan (*mishpahah*), composed of closely related father's houses tracing blood lines to a common ancestor several generations back. Here the members shared stories, traditions, and education. The clan was a good place to find a spouse, but also for rivalries. Extended families that lived in close proximity to each

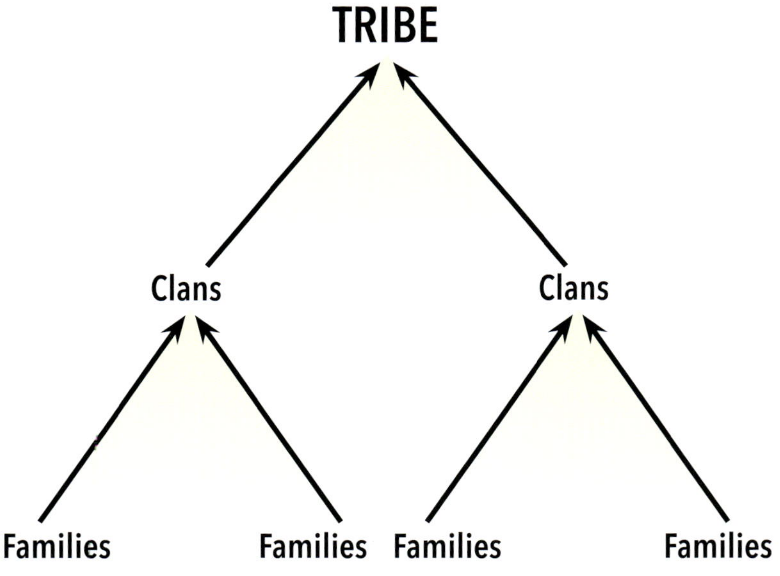

other and shared resources (fields and water sources) formed villages governed by family elders. Here extended families built cooperative frameworks for cultivating, harvesting, producing crafts, organizing and regulating water resources, and defense. Religious celebrations, local traditions, and mutual aid all centered on larger family and village communities.

The largest unit was the tribe (*shevet* or *matteh*), a group of related villages united for economic strength and mutual defense (Judg. 5:12–18). Each Israelite tribe took the name of its founding ancestor, one of the sons or grandsons of the patriarch Jacob (renamed Israel).

At every level of ancient Israel's social structure all plans and actions were aimed at strengthening, providing for, and protecting the well-being of the family. Together these brought honor. Honor was especially valued when bestowed on those who could not easily care for themselves within the family structure, namely the very young, the elderly, the infirm, widows, orphans, and foreigners. Anything that weakened the family or its reputation brought shame, something that could continue for generations.

DAILY LIFE AND WORK

Men and women together were tasked with providing for and protecting the family's viability and honor, and both were empowered to do so. Men tended to focus on outdoor work in the fields, orchards, or with the flocks; negotiated agreements within or between families, clans, or tribes; and fought in wars when necessary. The daily tasks related to running the household (the basic economic and social unit of society) were performed by women. In addition to keeping everything going, they were responsible for teaching skills and values to the next generation. Having many children was a blessing (though infant and childhood mortality was frightfully high), but so was old age, for it brought wisdom that surpassed the busyness and trials of the day. All-in-all, ancient Israel's social structure was a clearly defined and time-tested way of surviving in a difficult and unpredictable land. When done properly, it brought honor to the household, fostering values that served to stabilize life in times of famine or invasion.

Because the Israelites entered Canaan after forty years of living in the desert, their earliest houses were goat-hair tents. These tents were fully adapted to both heat and rain and allowed the family to set up seasonal campsites wherever grazing was best. Each tent housed a family unit, with closely related families pitching their tents near each other. Life in tents was so foundational for ancient Israel that centuries later, when many Israelites lived in cities, Isaiah likened their expanding kingdom to building a bigger tent (Isa. 54:2).

Once the Israelites entered Canaan, they began a long transition from living a seasonal, semi-nomadic life to settling in permanent locations, slowly replacing their tents with mudbrick or stone structures—and they also used natural caves as living spaces in the hilly areas. There was always sheltered space for livestock within the housing compound so that the family's animals (an important sign of wealth) could be protected from harm and in turn provide readily accessible products

Remains of a four-room house at Tel Gezer, west of Jerusalem.
This house dates to the 8th century BC and was likely destroyed in the Assyrian invasion.

for clothing, food, and fuel (1 Sam. 28:24). At harvest time, families lived out in the fields in structures that doubled as watchtowers, or slept on threshing floors to ensure that no one would snatch the hard-earned reward of their toil—for instance, Ruth visits Boaz as he slept "at the far end of the grain pile" on the threshing floor (Ruth 3:6–7).

Israelite homes were built according to a floor plan that archaeologists call a "four-room house." This involved positioning three rectangular rooms in a U-shape around a shared interior space, the fourth room, which provided direct access to the outside. If the family was large, the rooms were subdivided or there was a second story. Public activities such as hosting visitors took place near the entrance of the house, while private activities within the family happened close to the rear in what the Bible calls "the innermost part of the house" (Ps. 128:3; Amos 6:10 NASB). Each of the three rooms had direct, equal access to the shared, center space for common activities such as grinding grain, cooking, eating, and socializing. This arrangement allowed private space for subgroups within the household: the patriarch and matriarch with their small children, the oldest son with his wife and children, or those who were required to temporarily remain apart from the rest of the family in line with ritual purity laws.

FOOD AND MEDICINE

The ancient Israelite diet was largely limited to what was grown or produced locally, and this varied based on where individual families lived. People living in desert areas survived primarily on dairy products produced by sheep and goats, bolstering their diet from plants foraged from the desert. Because slaughtering animals would otherwise deplete the flock, meat was reserved for special occasions, such as weddings, hosting important guests, or celebrating religious festivals. Grubs, insects, and other creeping things were also a readily available mainstay of protein. Some, such as locusts, were even considered ritually clean (Lev. 11:22). Given the ever-present realities of hunger, we cannot assume that all Israelites scrupulously kept the Levitical dietary laws.

Families living where the annual rainfall was over 12 inches (300 mm) typically kept flocks, although the mainstay of their diet came from crops. There were two growing seasons:

- Wheat and barley were planted in the autumn with the onset of the annual rains and harvested in late spring and early summer after the rain ended.
- Orchard and vineyard crops (grapes, figs, pomegranates, olives, and dates) ripened from late summer through the autumn.

All produce, as well as meat and dairy products, could be dried, salted, or otherwise processed so that they could be eaten throughout the year. Given the scarcity of safe drinking water, these basic food groups also provided drink in the form of:

- milk from sheep and goats;
- a mildly fermented beer from grain; and
- wine from vineyards (recognizing this, the Bible gives strict warnings about drinking to excess; Prov. 23:20–21; 31:4–5; Isa. 5:22).

Natural sweeteners were dates, figs, and grapes. Almonds, legumes, eggs, and for some, fish, helped to round out the locally grown diet. The goal was to eat something from each of the main local food groups at least some of the time (1 Sam. 25:18; 2 Sam. 17:28–29). The primary

meal of the day was usually a thick stew of vegetables, lentils, or grain, rarely containing meat, eaten as sop with bread (Gen. 25:34; 2 Kings 4:38–39).

Villages located on the seams between fertile and arid lands, such as Bethlehem and Jerusalem, were market towns. There must have been lively economic and social activity here, as locally grown products and manufactured goods were readily exchanged between farmers and shepherds. The farmers provided grazing land after the crops were harvested, as well as fodder and fresh water; together, these were a hedge for shepherds against famine. Shepherds provided wool, milk, and meat, a hedge for farmers against famine. Transactions were through barter since coinage did not yet exist.

Shepherd tending her sheep in an olive grove between Jerusalem and Bethlehem

Medicinal potions, brewed at home from plant and animal products, were usually taken alongside prayers to God—or, for Israel's neighbors, the gods, since all polytheistic religions had a deity of healing (Isa. 1:6; 38:21; Ezek. 16:4; 30:21). Life expectancy was low (less than forty years on average), with the most critical transition being from birth to childhood. Even those who reached adulthood were constantly subject to illness, diseases compounded by insufficient diet, or debilitating accidents. Israelite medical practices generally lagged behind those of the urban centers in Egypt and Mesopotamia. In a very practical sense, this prompted the writers of the Bible to emphasize that the best remedy for illness was prayer to God (Deut. 7:15; Ps. 30:2; Isa. 38:1–5).

LANGUAGE

The Israelites and their neighbors spoke West Semitic languages, with the exception of the Philistines whose language was closely related to Greek. Scholars debate whether Hebrew derived from the language spoken by the Canaanites and Phoenicians or from the languages of the Ammonites, Moabites, and Edomites. Israelites living in different parts of the land developed local accents and dialects of Hebrew (Judg. 12:4–6). We can assume that the Israelites generally had no real trouble talking with each other or their neighbors, as indicated by the interactions between Joshua's spies and Rahab the Canaanite (Josh. 2); Jephthah and the Ammonites (Judg. 11); and Boaz and Ruth the Moabite (Ruth 2–3).

Though most people in the ancient world could not read or write, we do know of scribal activity (writing, reading, and record keeping) in the large Canaanite cities linked by international trade. Archaeologists have uncovered Canaanite religious texts. There is also some evidence that literacy was emerging in Israelite villages in the centuries before Israel became a kingdom. For instance, archaeologists have uncovered fragments of pottery and stone on which individual letters were written in alphabetic order (early Israel used the Canaanite alphabet), as well as short inscriptions indicating that objects were dedicated to a deity (sometimes to the Lord).

Oldest Canaanite full sentence, found at Tel Lachish. The writing is inscribed on an ivory comb (c. 1700 BC) and informs users that the object can "root out the lice of the hair and the beard."

The books of the Bible were most likely written by people trained as scribes, but virtually no one had their own copy, especially in the early centuries of Israel's settlement. With no easy access to written documents, there was little incentive for people to learn how to read and write. Most daily tasks, if not all, were learned orally, handed down from parent to child, expert to novice, teacher to student. This was also the case for learning the commands of God. When the Bible tells how people learned God's law (or Torah), it was almost always by listening to someone speak, not by reading it themselves; for example, "Joshua *said* to all the people, 'This is what the Lord, the God of Israel, *says*...'" (Josh. 24:2; emphasis added).

LEGAL MATTERS

The legal provisions in Exodus, Leviticus, and Deuteronomy provide a framework to shape the personal and social behavior of Israel. These laws were intended to guide, supplement, and in some cases replace, local legal traditions which the Israelites were already following. All in all, they were aimed more at restoration than punishment. They also placed a greater emphasis on fostering the welfare of everyone, including foreigners and not just the powerful, than did the legal traditions of Israel's neighbors.

At the village level, where most people were related by blood, conflicts between individuals or families were solved internally by elders who knew the perpetrators, the victims, and the specific issues at hand. The elders were respected heads of families whose authority came from the confidence placed in them by the community. Judgments tended to be based on precedence or local custom and applied on a case-by-case basis. The goal was to uphold and protect the rights of the ones harmed and restore broken relationships or at least make them tolerable enough for society to continue to function as best it could. The Bible mentions local legal traditions such as in Ruth 4:7, where a sandal is exchanged to ratify a transaction. Decisions were made at the entrance to the village at its gate if the village or city was walled (Deut. 22:13–15; Ruth 4:1; Jer 26:10), at the threshing floor (1 Kings 22:10), or in other open, public spaces where bribery, secrecy, and back-room deals would be more difficult.

Once Israel was ruled by a king, the need arose for more formal, comprehensive, written governmental and legal standards, created and enforced by authorities connected to the palace or temple rather than the village (1 Kings 7:7; 2 Chron. 19:4–11). The king's authority extended to imposing taxes and drafting people for military or public service, with these interests often overriding those of tribes, villages, and families, as the prophet Samuel had forewarned (1 Sam. 8:10–18; 1 Kings 9:15). Nevertheless, the final assessment of the turbulent period of the judges—"In those days Israel had no king; everyone did as they saw fit" (Judg. 21:25)—recognizes that elder law on the village level was also prone to abuse, and could be rectified by a single standard for people united at the highest level.

MARKING TIME

Time was based on seasonal, agricultural activities. For instance, Moses sent his twelve spies into Canaan when "it was the season for the first ripe grapes" (Num. 13:20); Samson visited his Philistine wife "at the time of wheat harvest" (Judg. 15:1); and Naomi and Ruth arrived in Bethlehem "as the barley harvest was beginning" (Ruth 1:22). Due to local variations in climate and soil conditions, planting and harvest times varied from place to place, putting each village or group of villages in slightly different "time zones."

The yearly calendar for everyone in the region was lunar, divided into twelve months, each marked by the appearance of the first crescent of the new moon. However, one unit of time that was unique to ancient Israel was the seven-day week. This is the only division of time that was not determined by natural phenomenon, such as the movement of the sun or

Crescent moon over the Arbel cliffs in northern Israel

moon and changes in weather. The week culminated in the Sabbath, a day when each Israelite was to step aside from daily activities to focus on the things of God (Ex. 20:8–11). Over time, keeping the Sabbath became perhaps the most visible mark of Israel's uniqueness among their neighbors.

RELIGIOUS ACTIVITY

Religious activity was an important part of the life for an Israelite, as it was for everyone in the ancient world. However, it is difficult for us to get a clear picture of what Israelite religious activity actually looked like, especially during the time of Joshua and the judges. This was long before the temple was built in Jerusalem when religious activity became centered there. The tabernacle and its priesthood were in Shiloh, but we have no indication how often most Israelites visited it, if at all. Joshua had warned the Israelites that even though they seemed eager to serve the Lord, they would quickly turn to the ways of their Canaanite neighbors when they settled among them (Josh. 24:14–24).

The Canaanites organized their deities in ways typical of pagan religions around the world. Each deity was a specialist who controlled a specific aspect of the natural world and to whom people turned for specific needs. Some were malevolent while others leaned toward benevolence, at least to an extent. Chief among them were:

- El, the creator and enthroned high god of ultimate control, though not particularly active in the daily affairs of the gods or people.
- El's consort Athirat (called Asherah in the Bible) who helped him subdue his god-enemies. As the prime goddess of fertility, Athirat, when in the mood, ensured that the land and its animals would be fruitful and multiply. In the Bible, she is represented as a sacred tree or a wooden pole (Judg. 6:26).
- Baal ("lord"), the divine alpha-male, a capricious and warlike fertility god who impregnated the land with rain.

- Baal's fertile sister-consort, Anath, a temperamental goddess of love and war.
- Yamm ("sea") and Resheph ("plague") who brought chaos to the world.
- Mot ("death"), the one to be feared most of all.

Canaanite gods were depicted as images (idols) which had to be appeased and cared for by priests, with the hope that the deities would return the favor and help those who acknowledged them. The biblical revelation that the one true God created and cares for his people freely, without needing to be enticed to do so, stands unique among the belief systems of all Israel's neighbors (Deut. 11:12).

Place names such as Beth Anath ("house of Anath") and Baal Hazor ("lord of the settlement") indicate that Canaanites maintained centers of religious activity throughout land that Israel settled (Josh. 19:38; 2 Sam. 13:23). Israelites eventually lived in these towns, but, tellingly, did not change their names. Archaeologists have found inscriptions mentioning the God of Israel alongside "his Asherah," clear evidence of the mixing of Israelite and Canaanite religion that the biblical authors so roundly condemned. Because the Israelites inherited the land of Canaan, they confronted the same day-to-day concerns that the Canaanites were facing, most notably the unpredictability of climate and rainfall that led to famine, plague, exile, or death. It is natural to expect that in the process, the Israelites were attracted to the long-standing religious worldview and activities of people who were already present there. The Canaanite religious views were persistent, seductive, and compelling for the Israelites, who were only in the process of learning about God and the covenant he made with them. The tide of mainstream culture was difficult to swim against, and the stories in Joshua, Judges, and Ruth provide examples of God's constant care as Israel endeavored to become more aware of his character and what wholesome lives lived under his command should be like.

As with all ancient peoples, Israel's neighbors believed in national deities—gods that were local to a particular territory and had divine sovereignty over the people living there. Chemosh was the god of the Moabites and Ammonites, Qos the god of Edom, Hadad the god of the Arameans in Damascus, Molech and Milcom also gods of the Ammonites, and so on.

The Israelite judge Jephthah, who may have been a good fighter but certainly was not a good theologian (or father!), seems to have believed that Chemosh gave territory to the Ammonites over which the Israelite God had no rights of interest or control: "Will you not take what your god Chemosh gives you? Likewise, whatever the LORD our God has given us, we will possess" (Judg. 11:23–24; see also 1 Kings 20:23).

Baal with raised arm (c. 14th–12th centuries BC)

When Ruth leaves Moab, it might be expected that she would change her loyalty to the deity of her new home in Israel (Ruth 1:16). Of course, as we finish reading the story, we find that Ruth comes to realize that there is more to following the Lord God of Israel than that switching allegiances.

As biblical revelation unfolded, the prophets were very clear that the territory of the Lord is universal: one God, one creator, one creation, and a single humanity which should acknowledge him (Isa. 44:24; 46:1–11; Jer. 16:19–21).

CHAPTER 7

Who's Who in Joshua, Judges and Ruth

Abdon

JUDG. 12:13–15

Abdon, the son of Hillel, led Israel as a judge for eight years. He had forty sons and thirty grandsons, each of whom had his own donkey, signifying Abdon's status and wealth. He was buried in Pirathon, which is in the land of Ephraim.

Abimelek

JUDG. 8:31–9:56

Abimelek was the son of Gideon and his Shechemite concubine. After Gideon's death, Abimelek, along with the Shechemites, murdered his seventy brothers to become king, even though he was not the rightful heir. He reigned over Israel for three years until the people of Shechem became disloyal, leading to a conflict. He was defeated during a siege of the city of Thebez, where a woman threw a millstone on his head, fatally injuring him (2 Sam. 11:21).

Death of Abimelek (Gustave Dore, 1866)

Achan

JOSH. 7:1–26; 22:20

The name Achan means "trouble." Achan was the son of Karmi, from the tribe of Judah. When the Israelites defeated Jericho, they were instructed to set aside all the riches for the Lord, but Achan stole some of these devoted items for himself and hid them in his tent. His disobedience led to the Israelites' defeat at Ai. When confronted about his sin, Achan confessed, and he and his family were put to death.

Adoni-Bezek

JUDG. 1:4–7

Adoni-Bezek's name means "Lord of Bezek." He was the ruler of Bezek, a Canaanite city in the north. At Bezek, the men of Judah and Simeon fought against the Canaanites and Perizzites, killing ten thousand of them. When Adoni-Bezek fled the battle, they captured him and cut off his thumbs and big toes. He recognized that this punishment was fitting because he had already done the same to seventy kings. He died in Jerusalem.

Adoni-Zedek

JOSH. 10:1–27

Adoni-Zedek was the king of Jerusalem during the Israelites' conquest of Canaan. When he learned that the city of Gibeon had surrendered to the Israelites, he summoned four other kings and their armies to attack Gibeon. When Israel came to Gibeon's aid, Adoni-Zedek and the other kings fled from the battle and hid in a cave, where they were trapped and subsequently executed.

Aksah

JOSH. 15:16–19; JUDG. 1:11–15

Aksah, the daughter of Caleb, was promised in marriage by her father to the man who captured the city of Kiriath Sepher. Othniel successfully captured the city, and Aksah became his wife. Aksah's father gave her land and springs of water.

Barak

JUDG. 4:6–22; 5:1–31

Barak was the son of Abinoam from Kedesh in Naphtali. The prophet and judge Deborah summoned him to lead an army against Sisera, the commander of King Jabin's forces. Barak agreed to do so only if Deborah accompanied him. She did, and he gathered ten thousand men to fight, thus ending twenty years of oppression.

Deborah and Barak Against Sisera
(Juan de la Corte, c. 1623–1642)

Boaz

RUTH 2:1, 4–16; 3:7–15; 4:1–13

Boaz, a righteous and prominent landowner in Bethlehem, was a relative of Elimelek, Naomi's deceased husband. Boaz married Naomi's widowed daughter-in-law Ruth, thereby redeeming the family property. He became the father of Obed, who was an ancestor of King David.

Caleb

JOSH. 14:6–15; 15:13–19;
JUDG. 1:12–15, 20

Caleb and the spies return with grapes from Canaan

Caleb, representing the tribe of Judah, was one of the twelve spies Moses sent to investigate the land of Canaan. Confident that God was with them, Caleb and Joshua gave a positive report. However, the Israelites ignored this message and received judgment as a result (Num. 13:1–14:38). Of the twelve spies, only Caleb and Joshua were allowed to inherit the promised land. Once in the land, Caleb received land in Hebron, as God had promised, but he first had to fight the land's inhabitants to claim it. He gave some of his land and springs to his daughter Aksah, who requested them.

Cushan-Rishathaim

JUDG. 3:7–11

Cushan-Rishathaim, whose name means "Cushan the Doubly Wicked," was the king of Aram Naharaim, a region in Mesopotamia. As a consequence of the Israelites' idolatry, God allowed Cushan-Rishathaim to oppress them for eight years. When the Israelites cried for deliverance, God raised up Othniel to defeat the king and rescue the people.

Deborah

JUDG. 4:1–5:31

Deborah, the wife of Lappidoth, was a prophet and judge in the hill country of Ephraim. She summoned Barak, informing him that the Lord commanded him to battle Sisera and the army of King Jabin. Barak agreed, but only if Deborah went with him. Deborah agreed to accompany him but told him that the honor of the victory would go to a woman instead. After King Jabin and Sisera were defeated, Deborah and Barak celebrated with a victory song, praising the Lord for his deliverance. Deborah's leadership was instrumental in Israel's deliverance, and she was called the "mother of Israel" (Judg. 5:7).

Delilah

JUDG. 16:4–20

Samson fell in love with a woman named Delilah in the valley of Sorek (presumably a Philistine). The Philistine rulers offered Delilah 1,100 shekels of silver to trick Samson into revealing the source of his strength so they could subdue him. She repeatedly urged him to disclose the secret, and he eventually complied, revealing that his strength came from his uncut hair, a symbol of his Nazirite vow. While he slept, Delilah arranged for someone to shave his head. With his strength gone, Samson was easily captured by the Philistines.

Samson and Delilah (José Echenagusía, 1887)

Eglon

JUDG. 3:12–25

Eglon, the king of Moab, formed an alliance with the Ammonites and Amalekites to wage war against Israel. Together, they conquered Jericho and oppressed the Israelites for eighteen years. In their suffering, the Israelites cried out to the Lord, who sent them Ehud, a left-handed Benjamite, to deliver them. Ehud killed Eglon, ending his oppressive reign over Israel.

Ehud

JUDG. 3:12–30

God raised up Ehud, son of Gera the Benjamite, as a judge to deliver the Israelites from King Eglon of Moab. Ehud brought a tribute to King Eglon and asked to meet him in secret. Ehud was left-handed, allowing him to conceal his sword on his right side and kill the king. After a daring escape, Ehud led the Israelites to victory against the Moabites, and the land experienced peace for eighty years.

Eleazar

JOSH. 14:1; 17:4; 19:51; 21:1–3; 24:33

The third son of Aaron and Elisheba (Ex. 6:23), Eleazar was a priest along with his brothers Nadab, Abihu, and Ithamar. After Aaron's death, Eleazar became high priest and faithfully served during the leadership of both Moses and Joshua. Eleazar commissioned Joshua as Moses's successor and was instrumental in overseeing the allotment of land to the tribes of Israel (Num. 27:18–23).

Elimelek

RUTH 1:1–3; 2:1–3; 4:3, 9

Elimelek, whose name means "my God is king," was the husband of Naomi and the father of Mahlon and Kilion. They lived in Bethlehem of Judah, until a famine struck the land. To escape the famine, Elimelek took his wife and their two sons to live in Moab, across the Dead Sea. There, in a foreign land, he died, leaving Naomi a widow.

Elon

JUDG. 12:11–12

The Zebulunite Elon judged Israel for ten years and was buried in Aijalon in the land of Zebulun.

Gaal

JUDG. 9:26–41

Gaal, the son of Ebed, led the people of Shechem in rebellion against Abimelek, the son of Gideon, but the rebellion failed.

Gideon

JUDG. 6:11–8:35

An angel of the Lord appeared to Gideon, the son of Joash, while he was hiding from the Midianites. God called Gideon to save the Israelites from Midianite oppression, but Gideon doubted his ability and asked for a series of signs to confirm his calling. With the Lord's enablement, Gideon went on to lead an army of 300 men to victory against 135,000 Midianites. Though the Israelites wanted to make Gideon king, he refused. Instead, he made an ephod, a religious object, which led Israel into idolatrous worship and became a snare for Gideon and his family. He was also known by the name Jerub-Baal, which means "let Baal contend with him."

Gideon Choosing His Soldiers (Gustave Dore, 1885)

Heber

JUDG. 4:11–24; 5:24

Heber was the husband of Jael, the woman who killed the commander Sisera. He was a descendant of Hobab, Moses's brother-in-law.

Ibzan

JUDG. 12:8–10

Ibzan of Bethlehem served as a judge of Israel for seven years. He had a large family, with thirty sons and thirty daughters. He arranged marriages for them with people outside the clan, reflecting his prominent status and efforts to form alliances with other tribes.

Jabin, King of Canaan

JUDG. 4:1–3, 17, 23–24

King Jabin of Canaan reigned from Hazor during the era of the judges (not to be confused with King Jabin from the time of Joshua). Jabin's army, led by Sisera, oppressed the Israelites for twenty years, until the Israelites under Deborah and Barak's leadership defeated his army.

Jabin, King of Hazor

JOSH. 11:1–15

King Jabin of Hazor reigned during the time of the Israelite conquest of Canaan. He led an alliance of northern kings against Joshua and the Israelites, but they were attacked and defeated at the Waters of Merom. Jabin was captured and then killed.

Jael

JUDG. 4:17–22; 5:2–31

Jael was the wife of Heber the Kenite. Her name means "wild mountain goat." When Sisera, the commander of King Jabin's army, fled a battle with the Israelites, he sought refuge in the tent of Jael because there was peace between him and her family. Jael welcomed him and offered him some milk. But when he fell asleep, she drove a tent peg through his temple and killed him.

Jael and Sisera (Hans Speckaert, 16th century)

Jair

JUDG. 10:3–5

Jair of Gilead judged Israel for twenty-two years. He had thirty sons, who rode thirty donkeys and controlled thirty towns in Gilead, which were called Havvoth Jair, meaning "settlements of Jair." When Jair died, he was buried in Kamon. Some believe that Jair of Gilead is the same Jair described in Numbers 32:39–42 and Deuteronomy 3:14, who was a descendant of Manasseh and captured a group of towns in Bashan, naming them Havvoth Jair.

Jephthah

JUDG. 11:1–12:7

Jephthah was the son of Gilead and a prostitute. He was driven from his home because of his illegitimate birth, but when the Ammonites attacked Israel, the leaders of Gilead asked Jephthah to return and lead them. As Jephthah prepared to battle the Ammonites, he vowed that if he were victorious, he would sacrifice whatever came out of his house to greet him. He was victorious, and his daughter, his only child, came out to greet him, which, of course, caused him enormous grief. Jephthah served as Israel's judge for six years.

Jether

JUDG. 8:20–21

As the firstborn son of Gideon, Jether was commanded by his father to kill the two kings of Midian: Zebah and Zalmunna. However, Jether could not carry out the task because he was young and fearful, so Gideon killed them instead.

Joash

JUDG. 6:11, 25–32

Joash the Abiezrite, from the tribe of Manasseh, was Gideon's father. Joash had an altar for Baal and an Asherah pole beside it, which Gideon destroyed in obedience to the Lord's command. Gideon built a new altar to the Lord on which he sacrificed his father's bull. When the people demanded that Joash kill Gideon for what he had done, Joash refused, declaring that if Baal was a god, he could defend himself.

Joshua

JOSH. 1:1–9; 5:13–6:27; 9:3–21; 18:1–10; 19:49–51; 23:1–24:33

Joshua, son of Nun, was Moses's successor and led the Israelites in the conquest of Canaan and the settlement of the land. He was one of the twelve spies sent to investigate Canaan. Because of his faith in God's promise that Israel would inherit the land, he and Caleb were the only members of their generation permitted to enter the promised land.

Under Joshua's leadership, the Israelites were victorious against significant Canaanite cities, such as Jericho and Hazor. However, his leadership faced challenges from the disobedience of Achan and the deception of the Gibeonites, which jeopardized the Israelites' successful conquest. Joshua played a crucial role in dividing the land of Canaan among the twelve tribes of Israel.

In his old age, Joshua assembled the people of Israel to renew their covenant with the Lord. He died at the age of one hundred ten, and he was buried in Timnath Serah, located in the hill country of Ephraim.

The name Joshua is connected to the Hebrew word *yehoshua* which means "the Lord is salvation" or "the Lord gives victory." The Greek form of the name Joshua is Jesus.

Joshua Passing the River Jordan with the Ark of the Covenant (Benjamin West, 1800)

Jotham

JUDG. 9:5–21, 57

The youngest son of Gideon, Jotham, hid during the massacre of his seventy brothers by Abimelek, allowing him to survive. Abimelek killed his brothers in an attempt to rule Shechem—a rule that his father, Gideon, had declined (Judg. 8:22). When Jotham heard that Abimelek was made king, he proclaimed a parable, rebuking the Shechemites from the top of Mount Gerizim. Then Jotham fled to Beer, where he remained, and later, God repaid the Shechemites for their wickedness.

King of Ai

JOSH. 8:1–2, 14, 23–29

When the Israelites attacked the city of Ai (perhaps the outpost guarding Bethel), they captured its king and hung him on a tree as God commanded.

King of Ammon

JUDG. 11:13–28

The king of the Ammonites claimed that the Israelites had taken his land when they came up from Egypt—a claim that Jephthah proved to be unfounded.

King of Jericho

JOSH. 2:2–3; 6:2

When the king of Jericho heard that Israelite men were spying on his land, he sent a message to Rahab, who fooled the king, claiming that the men had already left the city, though she was hiding them on her rooftop. The king was defeated by Joshua and the Israelites in the fall of Jericho.

Mahlon and Kilion

RUTH 1:1–5; 4:9–10

Mahlon ("sickly") and Kilion ("weakly") were the sons of Elimelek and Naomi, Ephrathites from Bethlehem in Judah. They died in Moab, leaving their Moabite wives, Ruth and Orpah, widowed.

Manoah and his wife

JUDG. 13:2–24; 14:2–10

Manoah, from the tribe of Dan, lived in Zorah with his wife (unnamed in the Bible). They were childless, but the angel of the Lord appeared to his wife and told her that she would have a son who would save the Israelites from the Philistines. Manoah prayed for God to send the angel again to instruct them on how to raise the child, and God answered that prayer. Manoah and his wife raised their son, Samson, as a Nazirite. When he wanted to marry a Philistine woman in Timnah, they objected to the marriage, but they were unable to deter him.

Manoah's Sacrifice (Frans Post, 1648)

Micah

JUDG. 17:1–18:31

Micah, who lived in the hill country of Ephraim, stole 1,100 shekels of silver from his mother. After hearing her utter a curse against the thief, he returned the money. His mother then gave him the silver to make an idol, which he placed in a shrine. Micah appointed his son as priest but later installed a Levite as priest. Eventually, the Danites stole Micah's idols and priest, an act that led the Danites into idolatry.

Naomi

RUTH 1:1–2:2, 18–22; 3:1–5, 16–18; 4:14–17

Naomi was the wife of Elimelek and the mother of Mahlon and Kilion. After the death of her husband and sons while living in Moab, she returned to Bethlehem with her daughter-in-law Ruth. Naomi, whose name means "pleasant," asked the women of Bethlehem to call her Mara, meaning "bitter," reflecting her loss and suffering. Naomi advised Ruth in her interactions with Boaz, and after Ruth and Boaz married, Naomi became a caregiver for their son Obed. Although Naomi's circumstances made her feel empty and bitter, God provided for her, bringing her fullness and joy.

Obed

RUTH 4:13–22

The son of Boaz and Ruth, Obed's birth served as a reminder of God's blessing and providential care. Obed became an ancestor of Jesse, the father of King David.

Oreb and Zeeb

JUDG. 7:25–8:3

Oreb and Zeeb were Midianite leaders of the army that was raiding Israelite villages and that fought Gideon and his men. The men of Ephraim captured Oreb and Zeeb, executing Oreb at a rock and Zeeb at a winepress. They brought their heads to Gideon.

Orpah

RUTH 1:4–15

Orpah was a Moabite who became the widow of Kilion, son of Elimelek and Naomi. When Naomi planned to return to her homeland, she instructed her daughters-in-law, Orpah and Ruth, to return to their mothers' homes. Orpah heeded Naomi's advice and remained in Moab, while Ruth chose to accompany Naomi to Bethlehem.

Orpah

Othniel

JOSH. 15:17–19; JUDG. 1:13–14; 3:7–11

Othniel was the son of Kenaz, the brother of Caleb. When Caleb led an attack on the people of Debir, he offered his daughter in marriage to the man who captured the city. Othniel successfully captured the city, so he married Aksah, Caleb's daughter. Later, Othniel became a judge of Israel, delivering the people from King Cushan-Rishathaim of Mesopotamia and securing peace for forty years until his death.

Phinehas

JOSH. 22:13–33; 24:33; JUDG. 20:27–28

Phinehas was the son of Eleazar and grandson of Aaron (Ex. 6:25). When the Israelites were in the wilderness, Phinehas killed an Israelite man named Zimri and a Midianite woman named Kozbi, ending a plague that God had sent to judge Israel for their idolatry and licentiousness. Because of Phinehas's zeal, he and his descendants were promised a lasting priesthood (Num. 25:7–13). In the land of Canaan, Phinehas and ten Israelite men investigated an unauthorized altar by the Jordan River. When the Israelites experienced an initial defeat in a civil war against the Benjamites, Phinehas received an oracle from the Lord that guaranteed Israel's victory.

Rahab

JOSH. 2:1–24; 6:17, 22–25

A Canaanite prostitute named Rahab lived in the city of Jericho. When two Israelite spies stayed at her house, she hid them to protect them from being discovered by the king of Jericho. Rahab announced her faith in the God of the Israelites. Because of her kindness to the spies, the Israelites spared her and her family from the destruction of Jericho, and then she lived among the Israelites.

Rahab and the Two Spies
(James Tissot, c. 1896–1902)

Ruth

RUTH 1:4–22; 2:2–3:18; 4:5, 10, 13

Ruth was a Moabite widow who loyally moved to Bethlehem with her mother-in-law, Naomi. Ruth began to glean in the field of Boaz, a wealthy relative of Elimelek, Naomi's deceased husband. Naomi encouraged Ruth to ask Boaz to act as their guardian-redeemer, which Ruth did, successfully. Ruth and Boaz were married, and through their son Obed, Ruth became an ancestor of King David.

Samson

JUDG. 13:1–16:31

Samson, a judge of Israel, was renowned for his extraordinary physical strength. Raised as a Nazirite, he was blessed and empowered by the Lord. Samson led Israel for twenty years during Philistine oppression, performing remarkable feats such as killing a thousand Philistines with the jawbone of a donkey and carrying away the massive gate of Gaza. His downfall came through Delilah's deception and his own foolishness, which led to his capture and eventual death while destroying a Philistine temple.

Samson's Wife

JUDG. 14:1–3, 7, 15–20; 15:1–6

When Samson saw a young Philistine woman in Timnah, he decided to marry her against the wishes of his parents. The men of Timnah forced her to manipulate Samson into revealing the answer to his wedding riddle, which enraged Samson, so much so that he killed thirty Philistine men. His wife was given to his friend, prompting Samson to burn the Philistines' fields. The Philistines retaliated by burning Samson's wife and her father.

Shamgar

JUDG. 3:31; 5:6

The judge Shamgar, the son of Anath, delivered Israel by killing six hundred Philistines with an oxgoad, a long, pointed stick used to drive livestock.

Sihon

JUDG. 11:19–26; JOSH. 2:10

King Sihon was an Amorite who ruled in Heshbon, which is east of the Jordan River. The Israelites asked Sihon to allow them to pass peacefully through his kingdom to Canaan, but he refused. As a result, God gave Sihon and his territory to the Israelites.

Sisera

JUDG. 4:2–22; 5:20–30

Sisera was the commander of the army of King Jabin of Canaan and was from Harosheth Haggoyim. Sisera commanded nine hundred iron chariots and for twenty years cruelly oppressed the Israelites. The Lord sent Deborah, a prophet and judge of Israel, to command Barak to lead ten thousand Israelites in battle against Sisera and Jabin's army. All of Sisera's men were killed in battle, and Sisera fled on foot. He sought refuge in the tent of Jael, but she killed him by driving a tent peg through his temple.

Tola

JUDG. 10:1–2

The son of Puah and grandson of Dodo, Tola delivered Israel and served as its judge for twenty-three years until his death. He was from the tribe of Issachar and lived in Shamir, located in the hill country of Ephraim.

Zebah and Zalmunna

JUDG. 8:4–21

Zebah and Zalmunna were kings of the Midianite army that Gideon attacked with only three hundred men. These two kings escaped with fifteen thousand men, a small fraction of their original army. Gideon and his men pursued, captured, and eventually executed these kings for their oppression of Israel.

Zebul

JUDG. 9:28–41

Zebul was the governor of Shechem and a deputy appointed by Abimelek, Gideon's son. When Zebul learned of Gaal and the Shechemites' rebellion against Abimelek, he warned him, allowing Abimelek to thwart the revolt.

Zeebl

See *Oreb and Zeeb.*

Zelophehad's Daughters

JOSH. 17:3–6

Zelophehad, from the tribe of Manasseh, had five daughters: Mahlah, Noah, Hoglah, Milkah, and Tirzah. He died in the wilderness before reaching the promised land. Because he had no sons, his daughters asked Moses to grant them the inheritance that belonged to their father. Moses agreed to their request at the Lord's instruction (Num. 27:1–8). Once they entered the land, Joshua fulfilled this promise, ensuring that the daughters received their rightful inheritance.

CHAPTER 8

Twelve Tribes of Israel

The twelve tribes of Israel were the family groups descended from the biblical patriarch Jacob (renamed "Israel"), the grandson of Abraham. God worked through these tribes to fulfill his purposes—especially his purpose of bringing from the tribe of Judah, Jesus the Savior, the Lion of Judah (Rev. 5:5).

- In the book of Genesis, we see God blessing and working through a family: Abraham and Sarah, then Isaac and Rebekah, and finally Jacob and his wives and their twelve sons who become the ancestral heads of the twelve tribes (Gen. 29:31–30:24; 35:16–18).
- Then God works through a nation: Israel—the descendants of Jacob's sons arranged into tribes. God brings them out of Egypt through the wilderness. At Sinai and during the forty years of wilderness wanderings after the exodus, the tribes camped around the tabernacle under their family banners. The priests and Levites camped on all four sides of the tabernacle.
- After the death of Moses, Joshua leads the tribes of Israel in the conquest of Canaan. Joshua distributes the land among the tribes as God had instructed.

> Their inheritances were assigned by lot to the nine and a half tribes, as the LORD had commanded through Moses. Moses had granted the two and a half tribes their inheritance east of the Jordan but had not granted the Levites an inheritance among the rest, for Joseph's descendants had become two tribes—Manasseh and Ephraim. The Levites received no share of the land but only towns to live in, with pasturelands for their flocks and herds.
>
> JOSHUA 14:2–4

The Family of Jacob (Israel)

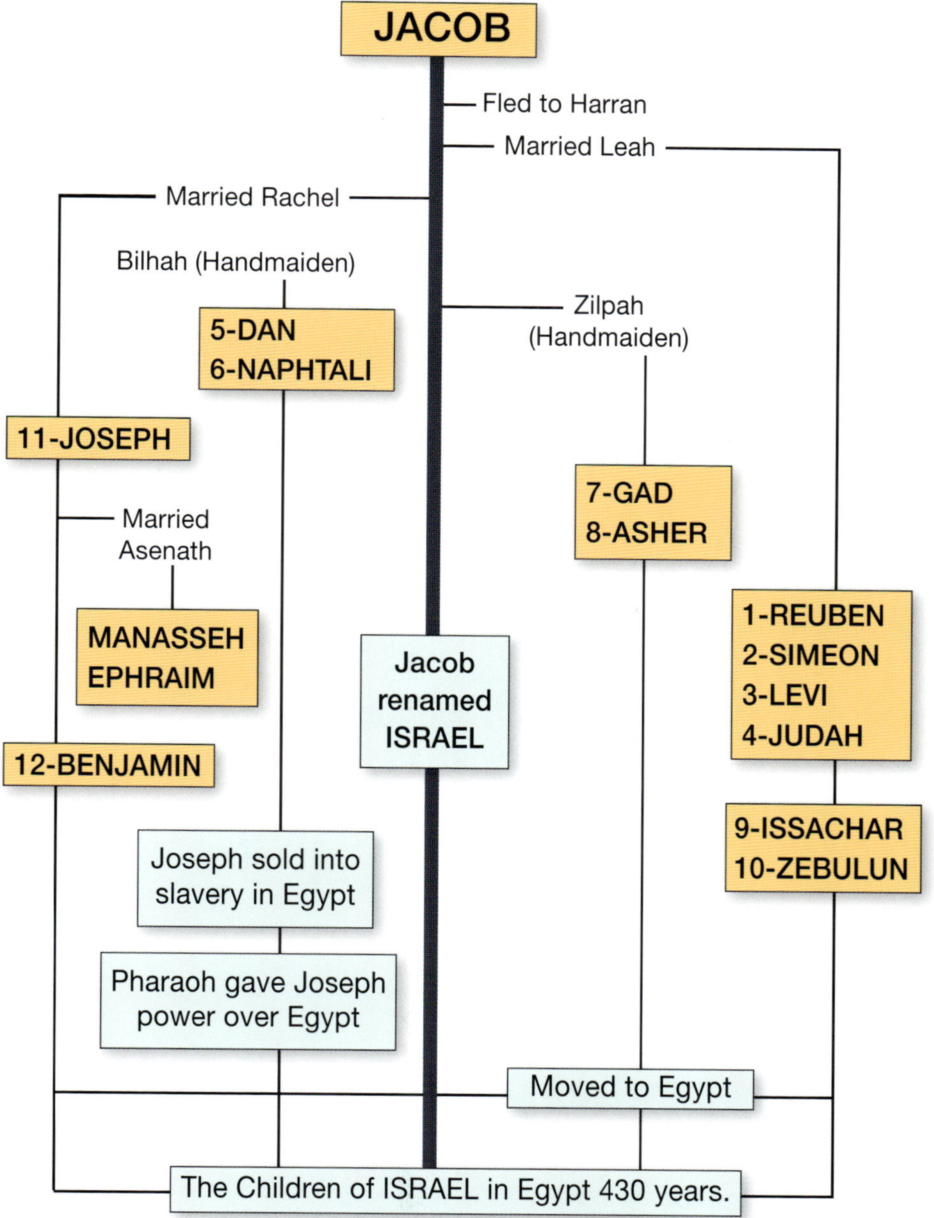

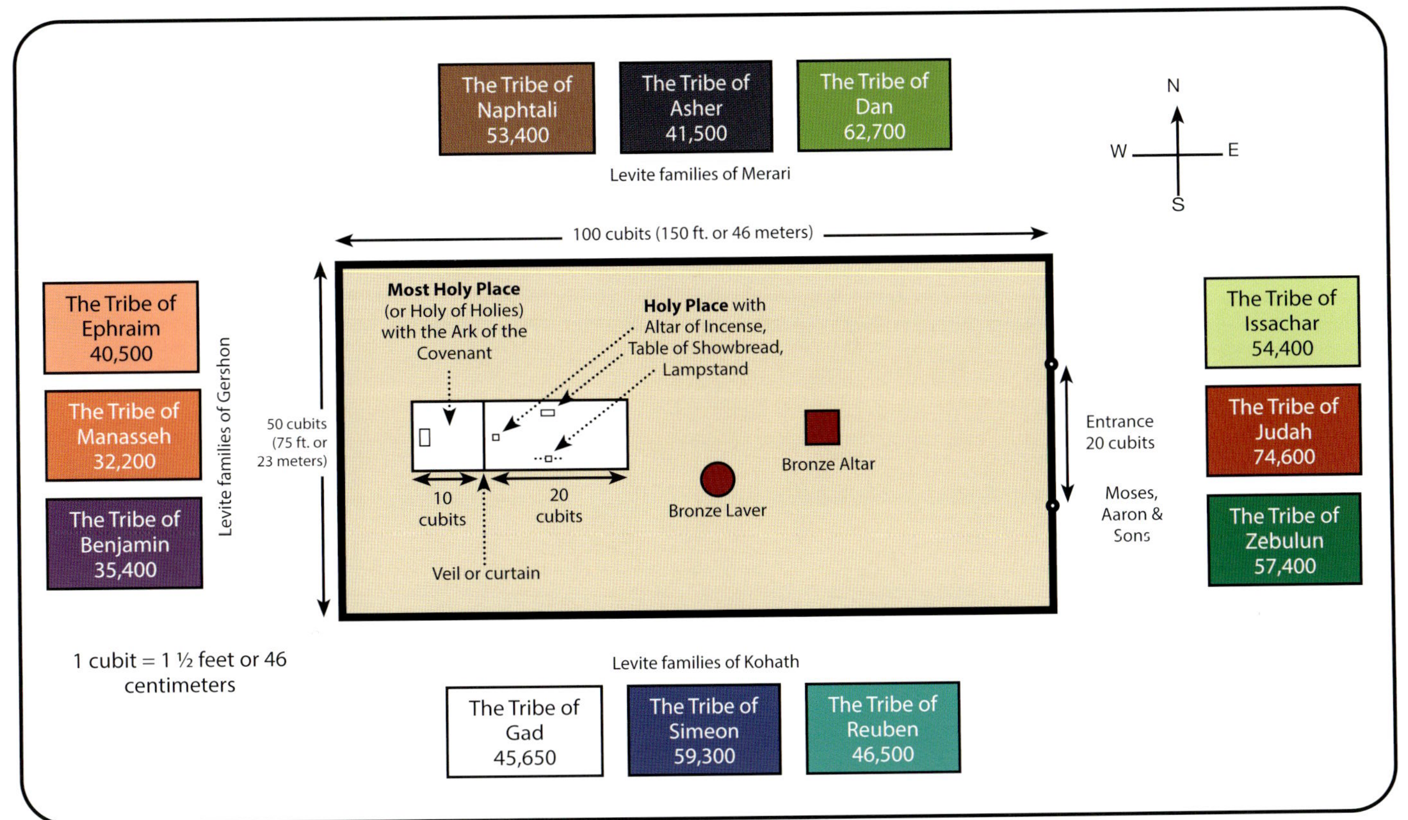

The figures shown here are from the first census, taken after Moses led God's people out of Egypt (Num. 1–3).

Breastplate of the High Priest

In the Old Testament, the high priest wore a breastplate made of linen and gold with twelve inlaid precious stones inscribed with the names of the tribes. Exodus 28:15–30 lists the stones right to left, as Hebrew is read right to left. The tribal names on the stones may have followed the order of how the tribes marched in the wilderness (Num. 2–3). Instead of Levi (the priestly tribe) and Joseph, the tribes of Joseph's sons—Manasseh and Ephraim—were represented on the breastplate. The exact identity and color of some of the tribal stones of the breastplate remain uncertain.

Zebulun	Issachar	Judah
Gad	Simeon	Reuben
Benjamin	Manasseh	Ephraim
Naphtali	Asher	Dan

Tribe symbols in this chapter are based on tradition and most reflect Jacob's blessings in Genesis 49. Bible scholars differ about the exact dates, meanings of names, tribal stones, and tribe locations.

REUBEN

Meaning: "See, a son!" (Gen. 29:32)

Symbol: Water (or mandrake plant; Gen. 30:14)

Stone/Color: Turquoise (or emerald)/greenish-blue

Family: First son of Jacob, born to Leah

Size: First census: 46,500. Second census: 43,730

Location: The tribe settled outside the promised land, east of the Jordan River in rich pasturelands suitable for their large herds and flocks (Num. 32:1); included Mount Nebo from which Moses viewed the promised land.

Jacob's Blessing: Jacob called his firstborn "my might, the first sign of my strength, excelling in honor, excelling in power." But Reuben had relations with Bilhah, Rachel's handmaiden (Gen. 35:22), so Jacob rebuked him saying that he is unstable as water and he will "no longer excel" (Gen. 49:3–4).

Moses's Blessing: "Let Reuben live and not die, nor his people be few" (Deut. 33:6).

Notable: Reuben intervened on behalf of Joseph to save him from being killed by his brothers. Nevertheless, when Reuben returned, he discovered that his brothers had sold Joseph to slave traders (Gen. 37). The tribe of Reuben kept their word by helping the other tribes conquer the promised land, though they themselves settled outside the land (Num. 32; Josh. 1:12–18). Yet at other times, they seemed indecisive and failed to assist in battle (Judg. 5:15–17).

SIMEON

Meaning: "Hearing"—God has heard

Symbol: Gate, like the gate of Shechem (or a sword)

Stone/Color: Lapis lazuli (or sapphire)/blue

Family: Second son of Jacob, born to Leah

Size: First census: 59,300. Second census: 22,200. Between the two censuses (a span of forty years) the size of the tribe significantly decreased. Though it is not clear why, it is possible that they suffered more severely than the other tribes from the plagues recorded in the book of Numbers (see Num. 25).

Location: The tribe received an enclave of land in Judah, likely with scattered settlements in Judah; included Beersheba.

Jacob's Blessing: Along with his brother Levi, Simeon attacked the people of the city of Shechem to avenge the assault on his sister Dinah (Gen. 34:24–31). Jacob rebuked Levi and Simeon saying, "Their swords are weapons of violence. Let me not enter their council ... for they have killed men in their anger.... I will scatter them in Jacob and disperse them in Israel" (Gen. 49:5–7).

Moses's Blessing: Moses does not mention the tribe of Simeon.

Notable: When Jacob's sons went to Egypt to buy food during a famine, Joseph imprisoned Simeon as a guarantee that Benjamin, their youngest brother, would be brought to Joseph (Gen. 42–43). The tribe was known for being shepherds, often migrating in search of pasturelands for their flocks, possibly a fulfillment of Jacob's prophecy that Simeon will be scattered and dispersed (1 Chron. 4:24–43).

LEVI

Meaning: "Attached"—Leah believed that having given birth to another son, Jacob would become attached to her.

Symbol: Breastplate of the high priest

Stone/Color: Not represented on the breastplate, but often associated with the tabernacle colors: gold, purple, blue, and red

Family: Third son of Jacob, born to Leah

Size: First Census: Not counted with the other tribes because they were caretakers of the tabernacle, not fighting men. They were counted separately and numbered 22,000. Second Census: 23,000.

Location: Joshua gave them forty-eight towns in the promised land in which to live and serve as ministers of the law among the tribes.

Jacob's Blessing: Along with his brother Simeon, Levi attacked the people of the city of Shechem to avenge the assault on his sister Dinah (Gen. 34:24–31). Jacob rebuked them for the attack (Gen. 49:5–7).

Moses's Blessing: "Bless all his skills, Lord, and be pleased with the work of his hands" (Deut. 33:11).

Notable: The priests were chosen from the tribe of Levi. Levites who were not chosen to be priests still participated in caretaking of the tabernacle (Num. 3:5–10). Once a year, on the Day of Atonement, the high priest wore the breastplate with the precious stones and entered the Most Holy Place of the tabernacle. He sprinkled a sacrificed animal's blood on the ark of the covenant to atone for the people's sins (Lev. 16). The Levites sided with the Southern Kingdom of Judah and migrated to Jerusalem after the Northern Kingdom rejected the Levites as priests (2 Chron. 11:13–17). When the Jews returned after exile, Ezra had to send a special delegation to persuade some of the Levites to return (Ezra 8:15–36). Moses, Aaron (the first high priest), Miriam, Ezra, Ezekiel, John the Baptist, and Barnabas were from the tribe of Levi.

JUDAH

Meaning: "Praise"

Symbol: Lion

Stone/Color: Carnelian (or ruby)/red

Family: Fourth son of Jacob, born to Leah

Size: First Census: 74,600. Second Census: 76,500. Judah was the largest of the tribes.

Location: The tribe received a very large allotment of land; included Jerusalem, Bethlehem, Hebron, and Gaza.

Jacob's Blessing: "You are a lion's cub, Judah; you return from the prey, my son. Like a lion he crouches and lies down, like a lioness—who dares to rouse him? The scepter will not depart from Judah, nor the ruler's staff from between his feet, until he to whom it belongs shall come and the obedience of the nations shall be his" (Gen. 49:9–10).

Moses's Blessing: "Hear, LORD, the cry of Judah; bring him to his people. With his own hands he defends his cause. Oh, be his help against his foes!" (Deut. 33:7).

Notable: Judah convinced his brothers to sell Joseph to slave traders for a profit instead of killing him (Gen. 37). Later, Judah unknowingly had relations with his daughter-in-law Tamar, and when it was revealed, he confessed his wrongdoing (Gen. 38). In the wilderness after the exodus, the tribe of Judah led the other tribes on their march toward the promised land. The tribe camped on the east side of the tabernacle—the only side with an entrance (Num. 2). Leaders like Caleb (a Kenizzite), David, and Zerubbabel were from the tribe of Judah, as were prophets like Amos, Micah, Isaiah, and Zephaniah.

DAN

Meaning: "Judge"

Symbol: Snake (or scales of justice)

Stone/Color: Topaz (or beryl)/color unknown, possibly light green

Family: Fifth son of Jacob, born to Rachel's handmaiden Bilhah

Size: First Census: 62,700. Second Census: 64,400.

Location: The tribe received a small portion of land that included Joppa (Tel Aviv today). The tribe, however, failed to conquer the Philistines in the land and migrated to the northernmost part of Canaan (Judg. 18).

Jacob's Blessing: "Dan will provide justice for his people.... Dan will be a snake by the roadside" (Gen. 49:16–17).

Moses's Blessing: "Dan is a lion's cub, springing out of Bashan" (Deut. 33:22).

Notable: The tribe of Dan is reprimanded in the Song of Deborah for not joining in battle (Judg. 5:17). Samson was from this tribe (Judg. 13:2, 24). King Jeroboam built a pagan temple in Dan (1 Kings 12:29). Amos includes Dan in his list of idolaters (Amos 8:14).

NAPHTALI

Meaning: "My struggle"

Symbol: Deer (doe)

Stone/Color: Jasper/reddish-brown

Family: Sixth son of Jacob, born to Rachel's handmaiden Bilhah

Size: First Census: 53,400. Second Census: 45,400.

Location: The tribe received the hill country of Galilee.

Jacob's Blessing: "Naphtali is a doe let loose; He bears beautiful fawns [or 'gives beautiful words'] (Gen. 49:21).

Moses's Blessing: Naphtali is "full of blessing" (Deut. 33:23).

Notable: In the Song of Deborah, the tribe is praised for its courage (Judg. 5:18). Barak was from Naphtali (Judg. 4:6). The tribe assisted Gideon in battle (Judg. 7:23). They volunteered fighting men to support David against King Saul (1 Chron. 12). Jesus began his ministry in Galilee, fulfilling Isaiah's prophecy (Matt. 4:13–22; Isa. 9:1–2).

GAD

Meaning: "Good fortune" (or "warrior")

Symbol: Tents, like a battlefield camp

Stone/Color: Emerald (or diamond)/possibly a stone with little color

Family: Seventh son of Jacob, born to Leah's handmaiden Zilpah

Size: First Census: 45,650. Second Census: 40,500.

Location: The tribe received fertile land outside the promised land, along the Jordan River (Num. 32).

Jacob's Blessing: "Gad will be attacked by a band of raiders, but he will attack them at their heels" (Gen. 49:19).

Moses's Blessing: Gad is commended for carrying "out the LORD's righteous will, and his judgments concerning Israel" (Deut. 33:21).

Notable: Gadites who supported David in his conquest of Jerusalem were described as "brave warriors, ready for battle and able to handle the shield and spear" (1 Chron. 12:8).

ASHER

Meaning: "Happy"

Symbol: Tree (or food)

Stone/Color: Onyx/black

Family: Eighth son of Jacob, born to Leah's handmaiden Zilpah

Size: First Census: 41,500. Second Census: 53,400. The tribe significantly increased between the censuses.

Location: The tribe received the northern coastal region along the Mediterranean Sea.

Jacob's Blessing: "Asher's food will be rich; he will provide delicacies fit for a king" (Gen. 49:20).

Moses's Blessing: "Let [Asher] be favored by his brothers, and let him bathe his feet in oil" (Deut. 33:24).

Notable: Asher is not included in King David's list of chief rulers, possibly indicating that by the time of David the tribe had lost its significance (1 Chron. 27:16–22). The prophet Anna, who recognized the infant Jesus as the Messiah, was from the tribe of Asher (Luke 2:36–38).

ISSACHAR

Meaning: "There is a reward"

Symbol: Donkey (or sun and moon)

Stone/Color: Chrysolite (or topaz)/yellowish-green

Family: Ninth son of Jacob, born to Leah

Size: First Census: 54,400. Second Census: 64,300.

Location: The tribe received the fertile Jezreel Valley, and their territory included Nazareth.

Jacob's Blessing: "Issachar is a sturdy donkey resting between two saddlepacks. When he sees how good the countryside is and how pleasant the land, he will bend his shoulder to the load and submit himself to hard labor" (Gen. 49:14–15 NLT).

Moses's Blessing: Mentioned along with Zebulun as tribes who will "feast on the abundance of the seas, and on the treasures hidden in the sand" (Deut. 33:18–19).

Notable: Deborah commended the tribe of Issachar for standing with the Israelites in battle (Judg. 5:15). During the time of David, the tribe was known for its wisdom: "men who understood the times and knew what Israel should do" (1 Chron. 12:32).

ZEBULUN

Meaning: "Dwelling"

Symbol: Ship

Stone/Color: Beryl (emerald)/possibly green

Family: Tenth son of Jacob, born to Leah

Size: First Census: 57,400. Second Census: 60,500.

Location: The tribe received a small portion of southern Galilee.

Jacob's Blessing: "Zebulun will live by the seashore and become a haven for ships" (Gen. 49:13).

Moses's Blessing: Zebulun and Issachar will "feast on the abundance of the seas, and on the treasures hidden in the sand" (Deut. 33:18–19).

Notable: Deborah commended this tribe for risking their lives (Judg. 5:18). They supported David with "undivided loyalty" (1 Chron. 12:33). When Hezekiah called for spiritual renewal, people from Asher, Manasseh, and Zebulun humbled themselves and traveled to Jerusalem (2 Chron. 30:10). Jesus began his ministry in Galilee—the land of Zebulun and Naphtali—fulfilling Isaiah's prophecy: "In the past he humbled the land of Zebulun and the land of Naphtali, but in the future he will honor Galilee of the nations.... The people walking in darkness have seen a great light; on those living in the land of deep darkness a light has dawned" (Isa. 9:1–2; see also Matt. 4:13–17).

JOSEPH

Meaning: Joseph: "He will increase." Manasseh: "One who forgets"—God made Joseph forget all his hardships (Gen. 41:51). Ephraim: "Double fruitfulness"—God made Joseph fruitful in the land of his suffering (Gen. 41:52).

Symbol: Sheaf of grain (or grapevine)

Stone/Color: Manasseh: Agate/yellowish-brown
Ephraim: Jacinth/orangish-red

Family: Eleventh son of Jacob, born to Rachel. Joseph's sons are Manasseh and Ephraim.

Size: Manasseh: First Census: 32,300. Second Census: 52,700 (the population greatly increased). Ephraim: First Census: 40,500. Second Census: 32,500 (the population decreased).

Location: The descendants of Joseph's two sons became recognized as two tribes and were given territory in the promised land. Manasseh received two large portions of land, east and west of the Jordan River. The eastern section was outside the promised land, and those in the eastern section are referred to in the Bible as the half-tribe of Manasseh. Ephraim received a small portion of land, which included Bethel where Abraham had built an altar (Gen. 12:8) and where God had confirmed the Abrahamic covenant with Jacob (Gen. 28).

Jacob's Blessing: Joseph is "a fruitful vine" (Gen. 49:22). Jacob blessed Joseph's sons saying that Ephraim would be greater than Manasseh the firstborn (Gen. 48).

Moses's Blessing: "May the Lord bless [Joseph's] land ... with the best gifts of the earth and its fullness" (Deut. 33:13–17).

Notable: Though Joseph was sold into slavery by his jealous brothers, God raised him to a place of prominence in Egypt. Joshua, Deborah, and Jeroboam were from Ephraim (Judg. 4; 1 Kings 12; 1 Chron. 7).

BENJAMIN

Meaning: "Son of the right hand"

Symbol: Wolf

Stone/Color: Amethyst/purple

Family: Twelfth son of Jacob, born to Rachel; she named him Ben-Oni, "son of my sorrows," as she was dying in childbirth, but Jacob renamed him Benjamin, "son of the right hand" which indicates a favored son (Gen. 35:18).

Size: First Census: 35,400. Second Census: 45,600.

Location: The tribe received a small portion of land just north of Jerusalem, a strategic position in ancient Israel.

Jacob's Blessing: "Benjamin is a ravenous wolf; in the morning he devours the prey, in the evening he divides the plunder" (Gen. 49:27).

Moses's Blessing: "Let the beloved of the LORD rest secure in him, for he shields him all day long" (Deut. 33:12).

Notable: In Egypt, Joseph tested his brothers by saying that he would keep Benjamin as his slave. When Judah pleaded with Joseph not to deprive his father of Benjamin, Joseph was moved to reveal his true identity and be reconciled with his brothers (Gen. 44–45). In the era of the judges, a civil war nearly obliterated the tribe of Benjamin (Judg. 20). King Saul was from the tribe of Benjamin (1 Sam. 9:1–2). After Saul's death, the tribe fought against David for control of the kingdom but eventually sided with David (2 Sam. 2). Jeremiah, Mordecai, and the apostle Paul were from the tribe of Benjamin (Jer. 1:1; Est. 2:5–6; Phil. 3:5).

THE TRIBES IN THE NEW TESTAMENT

The genealogy in the gospel of Matthew shows how Jesus was a descendant of the tribe of Judah through the royal lineage of King David (Matt. 1; see also Ps. 89:3–4; Isa. 9:6–7; Heb. 7:14). Jesus the Messiah was born in Bethlehem of Judah as Micah had prophesied:

> But you, Bethlehem Ephrathah, though you are small among the clans of Judah, out of you will come for me one who will be ruler over Israel, whose origins are from of old, from ancient times.
>
> MICAH 5:2

In the Gospels, we see God working through a different group of twelve: Jesus's twelve disciples. They spread the good news of salvation and performed miracles with the authority of Jesus (Matt. 10:1–4).

> Jesus called his twelve disciples to him and gave them authority to drive out impure spirits and to heal every disease and sickness.
>
> MATTHEW 10:1

In the book of Revelation, the apostle John recounts his vision of 144,000 people—12,000 from each of the twelve tribes—sealed with God's name (Rev. 7; 14:1). In his list, John leaves out Dan and Ephraim (a son of Joseph) but includes Joseph and Manasseh (Joseph's other son). This list is different than any other biblical list of the tribes. For instance, the list in Ezekiel 47–48 includes all the tribes who were given portions of land when the Israelites entered the promised land. John's unusual list of tribes leads some Bible scholars to suggest that the 144,000 represent all believers in Jesus, instead of a literal number of Jewish believers. (See James 1:1 where James may be addressing believers as the "twelve tribes scattered among the nations.")

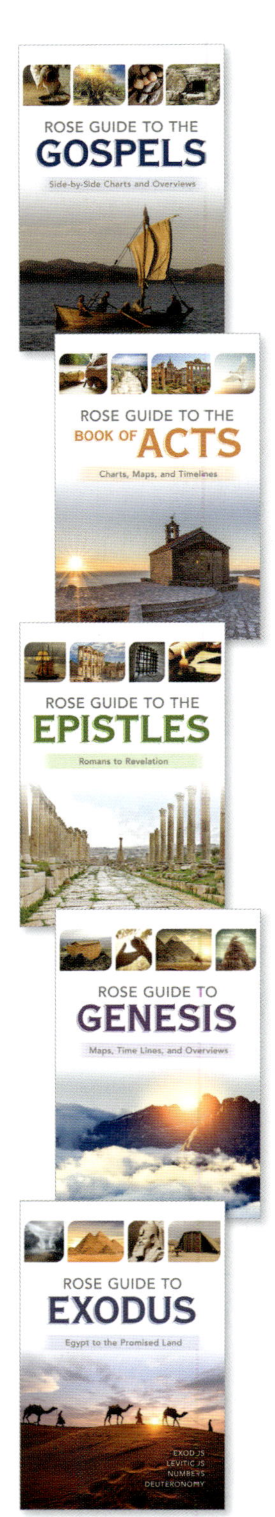

Rose Guide to the Gospels

Includes: key information about the uniqueness of each gospel; a harmony of the gospels; who's who in the gospels; background to the world of Jesus; evidence for the resurrection.

ISBN 9781628628111

Rose Guide to the Book of Acts

Includes: overview of the book of Acts; understanding the message and background of Acts; life of the apostle Paul; who's who in Acts; time line and maps; the Holy Spirit in the lives of Christians.

ISBN 9781649380203

Rose Guide to the Epistles

Includes: overview of the epistles; key facts on each epistle at a glance; who's who in the epistles; the seven churches of Revelation; comparison of Christian views on the book of Revelation.

ISBN 9781649380227

Rose Guide to Genesis

Includes: charts, maps, and time lines for the book of Genesis; stories of Noah's ark, Abraham, and Joseph; understanding the ancient world; who's who in Genesis.

ISBN 9781496477996

Rose Guide to Exodus

Includes: life of Moses; when and where the exodus occurred; the tabernacle and the ark; Passover and other feasts; the Ten Commandments.

ISBN 9781496484598

rose-publishing.com